From Karma
to
Grace

From Karma
to
Grace

The Power of the Fruits of the Spirit

John Van Auken

A.R.E. Press   •   Virginia Beach   •   Virginia

A.R.E. Press
215 67th Street
Virginia Beach, VA 23451-2061

ISBN-13: 978-0-87604-495-7 (trade paper)

Cover design by Christine Fulcher

Contents

1

Karma

The word karma originated in the ancient Indo-Aryan language of Sanskrit, which is the religious language of Hinduism and Buddhism. It comes from a root word that means "to do, to make." The broader meaning of this term is that thoughts, spoken words, and physical actions create a response in both the macrocosm of the outer life and the microcosm of the inner life of an individual soul. Even the most private thoughts, words, and actions generate a reaction as well as make an impression on an ethereal film of the collective consciousness, what is referred to as the *akasha* in Hinduism, which is comparable to the Western concept of the "Book of Life" for each soul and, in metaphysical circles, often called the akashic record.

Interestingly, when Edgar Cayce would enter a deep, meditative trance to read the akashic record, he explained that thoughts were as real as actions, so much so that he had to strain to determine whether the soul seeking the reading actually *did* something or just *thought* about doing it. In the greater scheme of life, especially soul life, thoughts are as real as actions. Here are two of Cayce's readings on this matter:

> The Mind—which is of the earth earthy but of heaven heavenly, and divine—is the *builder,* and so the thoughts may become crimes or miracles depending upon how they are applied in the experience of each soul in its sojourn through any period of activity in the earth. But, as has been intimated, know that the thought of a soul influences the sun, the moon, and all the heavenly hosts; for as you do unto the least of your brethren you do it unto the Creator. O that men would learn, would become conscious, that as you think of those—even though they beguile you, though they deride you, though they tamper with your own purpose—as you do unto them, you do it unto God. EC 315-4

> For mind is the builder and that which we think upon may become crimes or miracles. For thoughts are things and as their currents run through the environs of an entity's experience these become barriers or steppingstones.   EC 906-3

In Hinduism (originating approximately 7000 years ago, or millions of years ago, according to the *Ramayana*), the word *karma* first appears in the Rig Veda, the oldest portion of the Vedas, which are the religious texts of Hinduism. Veda means "knowledge." Rig Veda means "knowledge in verse" and is a collection of poetic hymns written some 3700 to 3300 years ago. In the Rig Veda, karma means "religious sacrifice." Curiously, there is no suggestion in the Rig Veda of its later meaning as a reactive force affecting a soul's character and circumstances. There is some indication of this in the Upanishads (another portion of the Vedas, written roughly 2800 to 2400 years ago). Here it is taught that action creates tendencies in a soul, which then produce further action, and as a result, further reaction, or karma. According to these teachings, the soul's subtle body (the "vehicle of consciousness"; *sukshma sarira* in Hinduism) carries the seeds of karma, and the physical body and world are the fields in which the reaction is experienced. Hence more karma is also created, which generates a recurring cycle of birth, death, and rebirth for the soul. The soul becomes caught up in a cycle of action and reaction.

Vedanta (another part of the Vedas) and Yoga (six distinct Hindu philosophies) speak of three kinds of karma: (1) karma to be experienced during the present lifetime, (2) the karma sown in the present life and reaped in a future life, and (3) latent karma, or the carry-over of karma to be experienced at some point when the stimulation is just right to bring it to the surface again. Liberation (*moksha*) is freedom from karma. When liberation is attained, the great storehouse of latent karma is burned up and present-life karma is resolved. The liberated soul creates no new karma and, at death, having no more karma, is no longer caught in the wheel of birth, death, and rebirth.

The idea that latent karma can be dissipated in the fire of enlightenment is fundamental to this book's intention. The fire we are speaking of is that which cleanses consciousness, purges negative habits, and purifies intentions. This is not only an Eastern but a Western teaching, also found in Western Scripture and teachings, as exemplified in these quotations:

> Our God is a consuming fire.
>
> Hebrews 12:29

> I baptize you with water for repentance, but he who is coming after me . . . he will baptize you with the Holy Spirit and with fire.
>
> Matthew 3:10

Fire is often a metaphor for the Spirit, especially the cleansing Spirit that burns up karma and its reappearing influences, leaving one renewed and strong. In this book we will study the "Fruits of the Spirit," which are those practices and dispositions that contain the seeds of the Spirit and, when enlivened through application in our daily lives and nurtured in our innermost being, ignite the cleansing Spirit. We will also learn about the magical power of Grace and its role in our soul growth and mental enlightenment.

Fundamental to the teaching of karma is the responsive nature of thought, word, and action. The motivating influence generating thoughts, words, and actions creates a corresponding response. If the intention is in harmony with the Creative Forces, then so-called good karma results. If the intention is destructive or out of harmony with the universal life force and the ideal pattern for all life, then bad karma results.

It is important to understand that the response is neutral; in other words, it is without passion. A simple universal law governs it: Whatever we do with our free will—in thought, word, or action—comes back upon us. The response is not motivated by retribution or punishment but by the Grace of the Divine to educate and enlighten. The law is intended to help the doer better grasp his or her effect upon self, others, and the whole of creation.

We express our knowledge of this law when we say "what goes around comes around" and "be careful what you wish for." In our sacred Scriptures we find: "An eye for an eye"; "As you sow, so shall you reap"; and "With what measure you measure, so shall it be measured to you." These sayings articulate the law of karma. Even scientists observe that for every action there is an equal and opposite reaction.

The law is unavoidable and immutable. Jesus taught that not one jot will be erased from the law and warned that those who teach otherwise are deceiving themselves and others. (Matthew 5:18)

There is an old saying whose origin is lost in antiquity, but Tryon Edwards, a theologian in the 1800s, republished it. It reveals the creative process of karma:

> Watch your thoughts, for they become words.
> Watch your words, for they become actions.
> Watch your actions, for they become habits.
> Watch your habits, for they become character.
> Watch your character, for it becomes your destiny.

We are what we have thought, spoken, and done. Our destiny is the karma of our previous thoughts, words, and actions; but more than that, it is a habit pattern that we are building. And, as with most habits, it will be difficult to stop. Our motivations, expectations, and concerns (even fears) shape our inner and outer reality. Fortunately, the law is ever in effect, and therefore we can change our tomorrows and our character by engaging better thoughts, words, and actions today.

Karma does not always result as an immediate response. It may lie dormant within the heart and mind and on an etheric fabric of the collective consciousness until some stimulant awakens it. Often this response comes in a future experience and new setting, possibly even with different souls from those with whom it originated, although it is more likely that they are the same souls but with new personalities in different settings. The outer self often feels unfairly put upon, having no memory of the origins of these responses, habits, and character traits. And although they are innate, the outer self rarely comprehends their presence, because karma belongs to the deeper self, the soul self. In one respect, karma is deep memory, within both the individual and the collective memory. Since the outer mind is often focused on current situations, it does not see the whole of soul life and soul karma—it lives on this side of a veil that separates inner consciousness from physical consciousness. In some ways this is a blessing because it removes the weight of guilt, fear, and self-condemnation. In other ways it is painful and confusing because the outer self cannot understand why these things are happening and where its poor habits come from. But the lesson to be learned is not so much for the outer, earthly self but for the inner, eternal soul, and the soul learns through the senses of the outer self. Of course, if the outer and inner selves have made progress toward cooperation and reunion, then both may know and understand what is going on—and the veil that separates them becomes less opaque.

When thinking of karma, it is important to realize that its influence is not only in the deeper consciousness but also inside the physical body, in the "mind" of the body's cells, tissues, and organs, or what is often called "body memory." The incarnating soul brings its karma with it and distributes its influence throughout the body as it enters at birth into the nervous systems (cerebrospinal and sympathetic-parasympathetic, which correspond to the Yogic sushumna and ida-pingala) and the endocrine glands (which correlate with the chakras and lotuses). The incarnating soul influences the genes of the physical body, turning on certain genes while leaving others off, and this may change throughout the incarnation. How one attends to the physical temple of the soul affects the temple's condition, both now and in the future. Good health is often good karma. Poor health is often a result of bad karma—though not always, as we shall see later.

Why is there a universal system of cause and effect? The metaphysical answer is that the original, infinite, immortal, perfect consciousness burst into creative expression and then allowed the creation to unfold freely as it expanded. It conceived of countless points of consciousness within its universal consciousness, giving each free will. The universal consciousness knew the potential for disharmony, confusion, and even chaos . . . but also the wondrous potential for joy, love, and enlightenment. In order to keep the creative process from spinning completely out of control, a simple law was established: Free-willed expression must know the consequences of expression. The Creator imbued each individual consciousness with an inner sense of the ideal universal condition. The law helps each entity to adjust its motivations, behavior, and character development as it learns from the consequences of its thoughts, words, and actions. The deeper mind is the builder, and it is always correlating thoughts, words, and actions with the ideal established by the Creator—seeking to ultimately be a companion to the Creator, thus striving to become companionable and in harmony with the ideal.

All of this becomes difficult to grasp when perceived from a finite, temporary perspective. Soul life is on a much grander scale and timeless, as compared to one eighty-to-a-hundred-year incarnation. And yet the soul's opportunity for resolving karma lies within the choices, behavior, and character development of the present incarnation. The finite experience is an opportunity to improve the infinite, eternal experience.

In day-to-day physical life, we easily forget that we were created to be companions and co-creators with the infinite First One, the Creator, out of whom all originally found life and consciousness. God created us in love to know each other and share life. In order to realize this, God gave us free will, the ability to independently choose to be companions. Without free will, we could only become children, subordinates, automatons, or loving servants but not true companions. . . companions choose to be with you and commit through thick and thin, in good times and bad.

Before the gift of free will was given, God set up a simple yet powerful universal law—Whatever one does with free will, one will experience—not as punishment or retribution but as education and enlightenment, that one may know the effects of one's thoughts, words, and actions.

How, then, can any of us survive our mistakes with free will? Who has not misused free will? Are we now caught up in a tangled web of karmic reactions to our prior misuses of free will? Not necessarily. Jesus said that the Spirit seeks mercy from us, not sacrifice. When He taught this lesson, He said that curious little saying of His, "He who has ears to hear, let him hear." It's as though there is some secret within these words, "I seek mercy, not sacrifice." (Matthew 9:13 and 12:7) The secret is that the law is so perfect that we do not have to make up for all our past sins with free will; rather, we have to understand these mistakes in others who have and do misuse their free will. The law is absolute: What you do or think comes back upon you. If you can understand the misuse of free will in another, then it is understood in you! If you can forgive the misuse of free will by another, then it is forgiven in you. And, best of all, if you can *forget* the misuse of free will by another, then it is forgotten in you. This is the secret in Jesus' words, "I seek mercy, not sacrifice." Few of us could sacrifice enough to make up for our misuse of free will, but having mercy upon others who have misused their free will brings mercy upon us. The law is absolute. Not one jot will be erased from it. Therefore, jots of understanding, forgiveness, and forgetting will also come back upon us.

With this understanding of karma established, it is now important for us to understand that not all of physical hardship and suffering is karma. Some is the test of the Spirit—actually, the test of Satan! In ancient Israeli teachings, Satan was the accuser (*ha-satan* in Hebrew, and the exact name used in the book of Job) and the tester, as we shall see in the story of Job. In fact, according to classical rabbis, Satan's job was to "break the barrel but not spill any wine." In other words, he is to test us hard but not destroy our soul in the process. In Kabbalah, Satan's role is to tempt us as best he can, then turn and accuse us when we fail—but the Kabbalists believed that, deep down, Satan wanted us to be victorious, because he was, in effect, an agent of God's testing. The planet Saturn and the day Saturday have been associated with the test by Satan. Astrologically, the planetary influence of Saturn is said to engage one in his or her tests on the way to self-awareness and enlightenment. Saturn's lessons require one to succeed through trials, building toward mastery of free will, God's gift to us. Here's the story behind the idea of a life with divinely approved tests and trials.

The high priest Melchizedek wrote the biblical book of Job for all incarnate souls to better understand the nature of incarnation. Life here is a test of our love, our companionability, and our commitment to God and the ideals that are Godly. Melchizedek begins the book by describing how the sons and daughters of God came together to present themselves before God, and Satan came among them. God turns to Satan and asks if he has seen the goodness in His servant Job. Satan challenges Job's apparent goodness, claiming that if God touched one thing of Job's physical life or physical person, Job would curse God to His face. Satan claims that the human is not interested in spiritual life with God, only physical life. He wants two cars in the garage, a chicken in the pot, a fantastic spouse, money in the bank, and a healthy body. Spiritual things are of no interest to him. Job's prayers to God are just to keep physical, selfish life the way Job wants it, not to awaken spiritually or know God personally. After Satan laid down this challenge, God instructed Satan to *test* Job to see if this were true. From that moment on, Job's physical life and body fell on hard times. His friends accused him of sinning against God or that members of his family had sinned. But Job insisted that every time he or his family sinned, he had asked for forgiveness, and Job believed that the all-merciful God forgave him and his family. Still, his friends wondered what else could explain these sufferings and misfortunes. Job had no answer to this question, but he did not and would not curse God. In the end, God and Job talked directly. They got to know each other and understand one another. A hundredfold of what Job lost in the test was restored to him.

So it is for all of us who journey through physical incarnation. Here we will be tested to see for sure what we really treasure: mammon or our Creator and ultimate companion. And the Spirit of God is composed of the Fruits of the Spirit. These fruits have the seeds of the Spirit within them and grow a more companionable soul to the Creator, who longs for our companionship. "God is a Spirit, and they that worship Him must worship in spirit and in truth." (John 4:24) What may be the qualities of this Spirit are revealed in the Fruits of the Spirit, the focus of study in this book.

God's wisdom is evident in this exactingly magical law of karma and the testing revealed in the book of Job. Understanding mistakes, vices, and weaknesses in others and faithfully enduring the tests are two keys to regaining our birthright as companions and co-creators with our Creator—the Creator of the entire universe and all that is in it.

2

Grace

Like karma, the word grace has its origin in the ancient Indo-Aryan language of Sanskrit. It comes from the root words *gr* and *grnati*, meaning "warm approval" and "favorable acceptance," respectively. It finds it way into Latin as *gratia*, meaning "to favor," and *ex gratia* means to give a favor when one is not required—this is where the word gets its greater meaning as an unmerited divine favor given to souls for their salvation, regeneration, and sanctification.

Although the effect of grace is similar to mercy, there is a subtle distinction: mercy is when God does not give us what we deserve, and grace is when God gives us what we do not deserve. Grace comes from God's awareness of our potential as eternal companions—the purpose for which God conceived us and gave us free will. Seeing this potential, God established leeway in the unfolding of creation and our soul growth. This leeway is the grace of God's love for us.

Aware of the ultimate potential of the developing soul, the Creator favors the soul even when it does not yet deserve it. Grace is a gift from the Creator to the created, given in a spirit of love and patience.

American writer and theologian Frederick Buechner wrote:

> Grace is something you can never get but can only be given. There's no way to earn it or deserve it or bring it about any more than you can deserve the taste of raspberries and cream or earn good looks or bring about your own birth.
>
> The grace of God means something like: "Here is your life. You might never have been, but you are, because the party wouldn't have been complete without you. Here is the world. Beautiful and terrible things will happen. Don't be afraid. I am with you. Nothing can ever separate us. It's for you I created the universe. I love you."

Grace is also with us because our Creator's presence is always with us, whether we are conscious of it or not. In conceiving us, our Creator made our deeper portion in its image, after its likeness, and placed a piece of itself within each of us. (Genesis 1:26–28) As a result, the Creator experiences what we experience, knows our most intimate feelings, and is aware of the temptations, tests, and karma that we face in our soul growth. This is beautifully expressed in Psalm 139:

> O Lord, you have searched me and you know me.
> You know my sitting down and my rising up.
> You perceive my thoughts from afar.
> You search out my path and my lying down, and are acquainted with all my ways.
> For there is not a word on my tongue, but, behold, O Lord, you know it altogether.
> You are with me, behind and before. You laid your hand on me.
> This knowledge is beyond me. It is lofty. I cannot attain it.
> Where could I go from your Spirit? Or where could I flee from your presence?

If I ascend up into heaven, you are there. If I make my bed
   in Hades, behold, you are there!
If I take the wings of the dawn and settle in the uttermost
   parts of the sea, even there your hand will lead me, and
   your right hand will hold me.
If I say, "Surely the darkness will overwhelm me; the light
   around me will be night;" even the darkness does not
   hide me from you, but the night shines as the day. The
   darkness is like light to you.
For you formed my inmost being, you knit me together
   in my mother's womb.
I will give thanks to you, for I am fearfully and wonder-
   fully made. Your works are wonderful. My soul knows
   that very well.
My frame was not hidden from you, when I was made in
   secret, woven together in the depths of the earth.
Your eyes saw my body. In your book [Book of Life;
   akashic record] they were all written, the days that
   were ordained for me, when as yet there were none of
   them.
How precious to me are your thoughts, O God! How vast
   is the sum of them!
If I would count them, they are more in number than the
   sand. When I wake up, I am still with you.

                              Psalm 139:1-18; brackets mine

Given our present physical reality and limited awareness, it is difficult to see how God is an integral and intimate portion of our being
and how we are a portion of God's being. God is with us, and this
naturally showers us with God's grace.

Elijah revealed this when he searched for God, after he had gotten
himself in trouble with the authorities and began to feel that he was
alone in his quest, and grew weary of his mission. At first, Elijah searched
for God in the things of power in the earth—thunder, lightning, fire, and
earthquake—but not finding God in these, he became quiet and
wrapped himself in his cloak, and there, within himself, he heard a

"still, small voice." At last, there was God's presence. God had been with him the whole time. In Psalm 46 God instructed the psalmist to "be still, and know that I am God." In Luke 17:11, Jesus taught, "the kingdom of God is within you." In Exodus 3:14, when Moses asked God for His name, God replied, "I am that I am," indicating that the great I AM is in that portion of us that has a sense of "I am." The great I AM and the little I am are one. Our little consciousness is a portion of the vast Universal Consciousness that is God's mind.

Jesus stated that no one ascends to heaven that did not first descend from heaven. (John 3:13) From our earthly perspective, this is an amazing statement, completely out of touch with our earthly reality. Yet Jesus, preparing to go to our heavenly Father, told Philip that he knew where He was going and that he, Philip, also knew the way! (John 14:4) Of course, Philip was confused by this statement, wondering how he could know the way to the Father and where the Father abides. He asked Jesus to simply show him the Father. We may ask, How can a portion of our being have known heaven and an intimate harmony with the Creator of the entire universe and have no present awareness of this? The answer is that our heavenly self abides on the other side of an opaque veil that divides earthly consciousness from heavenly. However, this veil is not permanent, and we can learn how to move through it, even eventually see through it regularly, uniting our inner and outer awareness. It is an intention of this book to help us diminish the opacity of this veil, making it transparent and no longer separating our heavenly self from our earthly self.

In addition to grace abiding with us because of God's awareness of our potential and God's ever-abiding presence, divine grace also accompanies every temptation, test, and karmic response! Our Creator has already prepared a way to overcome and resolve weaknesses, even in the worst of circumstances. For example, despite the clarity of the law of karma, reactions are rarely as exacting as the thoughts, words, and actions that generated the karma. This is because of God's gracious intention that the law not be used to punish us but to enlighten us. Even in the execution of the law we find divine grace giving allowance and favor.

In the biblical book of Zechariah, the high priest Joshua was brought before God, but Satan, always the accuser, pointed out how filthy Joshua's garments were, implying that Joshua's actions made him unworthy to be in God's presence. God's response is key to our understanding of grace motivated by love and a deeper awareness of our potential:

> Then he [the Lord] showed me Joshua the high priest standing before the angel of the Lord, and Satan standing at his right hand accusing him.
>
> And the Lord said to Satan, "The Lord rebuke you, O Satan! The Lord who has chosen Jerusalem rebukes you! Is not Joshua a burning branch plucked from the fire?"
>
> Now Joshua was standing before the angel of the Lord, clothed with filthy garments.
>
> And the angel of the Lord said to those who were standing before him, "Remove the filthy garments from him." And to Joshua he said, "Behold, I have taken your iniquity away from you, and I will clothe you with clean apparel."
>
> Zechariah 3:1-4

See how God extended favor to Joshua, even though he may not have deserved it? God even extended favor to the biblical archvillain Cain, saying: "Cain, why are you angry? And why is your face sad? If you do well, will you not be accepted? And if you do wrong, sin is waiting at the door [of your heart and mind], it seeks to possess you, but you must master it." (Genesis 4:6-7; brackets mine) Even after Cain murdered Abel, God protected him from revenge by others and allowed him to live and, it is hoped, learn.

Another important point in understanding grace is that the giving of grace reveals something about the nature of our Creator. Grace is a quality of God. In the Kabbalah's Tree of Life, one of the ten emanations of the Creator's presence is *chesed*, which is often translated as lovingkindness and mercy, grace-filled qualities of God. The Fruits of the Spirit contain the seeds of God's nature, and as we assimilate the fruits into our thinking, speaking, and doing, the Spirit grows within us until we and the Spirit are one. A most amazing effect of living with the abiding Spirit and thinking, speaking, and acting according to the abiding Spirit's influence is the *suspension* of the law of karma and the shift to a life in grace. In the life of grace, error does not result in karma to be experienced or lessons to be learned through suffering; rather, the Spirit instructs the soul from within, whispering guidance to the soul through its lessons. The lessons are learned within the heart and mind with the ever-abiding Spirit, not in the outer world of cause and effect, or karmic reaction. When the intention of the heart and mind is to do well, God seeks to strengthen and guide the soul in grace, not karma.

Edgar Cayce's visionary discourses explain this well, as in this quotation:

> Do that which is good, for there has been given in the consciousness of all the fruits of the spirit: Fellowship, kindness, gentleness, patience, long-suffering, love; these be the Fruits of the Spirit. Against such there is no law.
>
> Doubt, fear, avarice, greed, selfishness, self-will; these are the fruits of the evil forces. Against such there *is* a law. Self-preservation, then, should be in the fruits of the spirit, as you seek through any channel to know more of the path from life— from good to good—to life; from death unto life, from evil unto good. Seek and you shall find. Meditate on the fruits of the Spirit in the inner secrets of the consciousness, and the cells in the body become aware of the awakening of the life in their activity through the body. In the mind, the cells of the mind become aware of the life in the Spirit. The spirit of life makes not afraid.
>
> Then, know the way; for those that seek may find.
>
> EC 5752-3

In the next chapters we will explore the Fruits of the Spirit and learn how the law of karma becomes the liberating grace of soulful living.

3

Fruits of the Spirit

According to the disciple Paul, in his letter to the Galatians, the Fruits of the Spirit are love, joy, peace, long–suffering, gentleness, goodness, faith, meekness, and temperance. Here are his words:

> I say, walk by the Spirit, and you won't fulfill the lust of the flesh.
>
> For the flesh lusts against the Spirit, and the Spirit against the flesh; and these are contrary to one other, that you may not do the things that you desire.
>
> But if you are led by the Spirit, you are not under the law. [Note this statement, for it reveals the grace of a Spirit-led life.]
>
> Now the works of the flesh are obvious, which are: adultery, sexual immorality, uncleanness, lustfulness, idolatry, sorcery, hatred, strife, jealousies, outbursts of anger,

rivalries, divisions, heresies, envyings, murders, drunken-
ness, orgies, and things like these; of which I forewarn
you, even as I also forewarned you, that those who
practice such things will not inherit the Kingdom of God.

But the fruit of the Spirit is love, joy, peace, patience,
kindness, goodness, faithfulness, gentleness, and self-
control. Against such things there is no law. [Note again
how the Fruits of the Spirit lift one from the law.]

Those who belong to Christ have crucified the flesh
with its passions and lusts.

If we live by the Spirit, let's also walk by the Spirit.

Let's not become conceited, provoking one another,
and envying one another.

Galatians 5:16-26, WEB (World English Bible);
brackets mine

The American Standard Version (ASV) translates the ancient text with
a slight difference in two words: *patience* becomes *long-suffering* and *gentleness* becomes *meekness:*

But the fruit of the Spirit is love, joy, peace, long-
suffering, kindness, goodness, faithfulness, meekness,
and self-control.

ASV

The Revised Standard Version (RSV) interprets the wording exactly as
the World English Bible (WEB):

But the fruit of the Spirit is love, joy, peace, patience, kindness,
goodness, faithfulness, gentleness, and self-control.

Surprisingly, a major Catholic Bible translates this passage quite dif-
ferently from all Protestant translations, including the addition of three
new Fruits. This translation into English was a literal, word-for-word
translation of the ancient Latin Vulgate Bible, translated by Jerome from
the years 382 to 405. The Latin Vulgate was translated from Hebrew and

Chaldean Scriptures, which comprise the Christian Old Testament, and the Greek records of the Gospels, Epistles, and Revelation, which comprise the Christian New Testament.

This Catholic translation from Latin to English was published prior to the 1611 publication of the King James Version, upon which most modern Protestant Bibles are based. The Catholic English New Testament was first published in 1582 by the British College at Rheims. Later, in 1609, the British College at Douay published the Catholic Old Testament. Thus, this Bible is called the Douay–Rheims Version (DRV). Here is that most unusual translation.

> But the fruit of the Spirit is charity, joy, peace, patience,
> benignity, goodness, longanimity, mildness,
> faith, modesty, continency, and chastity.

Webster's dictionary defines *longanimity* as "forbearance," as in patient endurance, and *continency,* as the exercise of self-constraint in sexual matters. *Mildness* could easily correlate with "meekness." We have also seen that Paul's famous description of love in 1 Corinthians 13 has, in some translations, used the word *charity* for "love," expressing the selfless character of the type of love Paul was writing about. The word *benignity* reveals just how literal the translation was from the Latin, this word having the Latin root for *well-born,* which was believed to result in a manner and tone that was kind and gentle. *Chastity* is not listed in any of the modern non-Catholic translations. Somehow that got lost over the years, and the interpretation is rendered "self-control." Is it possible that this is temperance? Not likely, since we already have *continency* in the list, and *chastity* would mean abstinence, not moderation.

The most commonly published list of the Fruits of the Spirit contains nine fruits: love, joy, peace, long-suffering, gentleness, goodness, faith, meekness, and temperance.

In the Edgar Cayce discourses, *patience* is added, while maintaining *long-suffering,* as are *mercy* and *forgiveness.*

A blend of all these sources would produce this list:

The Fruits of the Spirit

Love
Mercy
Forgiveness
Patience
Faith
Meekness
Humility
Kindness
Gentleness
Peace
Joy
Goodness
Temperance
Long-suffering

It is this list that will be used in this book.

The Spirit of the Lord

Some consideration should be given to understanding what *Spirit* is. The first use of the term in connection with the Lord is found in the book of Numbers. In this passage, the Lord's Spirit came upon Moses in the form of a descending cloud. Moses had gathered seventy good men with him. The Lord took some of the Spirit that was upon Moses and put it on the seventy men. As a result, these men began to prophesy, but only while the Spirit was upon them. Here's the passage:

> And Moses went out and gave the people the words of the Lord; and he took seventy of the responsible men of the people, placing them round the Tent. Then the Lord came down in the cloud and had talk with him, and put on the seventy men some of the spirit that was on him; now when the spirit came to rest on them, they were like prophets, but only at that time.
>
> Numbers 11:24-25; Bible in Basic English (BBE)

The full term *Spirit of the Lord* does not appear in the Bible until the book of Judges. In this following passage, the people of Israel were in captivity and were crying to the Lord to deliver them.

> When the people of Israel cried to the Lord, the Lord raised up a deliverer for the people of Israel, who delivered them, Othniel the son of Kenaz, Caleb's younger brother. The Spirit of the Lord came upon him, and he judged Israel; he went out to war, and the Lord gave Cushan-rishathaim King of Mesopotamia into his hand; and his hand prevailed over Cushan-rishathaim.
>
> Judges 3:10

Othniel was the only judge in the Scriptures from the tribe of Judah. The name literally means "lion of God," Oth'ni–el. Interestingly, Jesus is referred to as the "Lion of the Tribe of Judah."

After this initial passage about the Spirit of the Lord coming upon the individual Othniel, the term appears over ninety more times in the Scriptures, including eight times in the New Testament.

In His local synagogue Jesus read a passage from Scripture before His townspeople, sat down, and then stated that today this passage had been fulfilled. Some who were present took this to mean that the Grace of the Lord was upon Him, while others questioned who He thought He was, speaking this way, because they knew Him as just the son of the carpenter Joseph.

> And he came to Nazareth, where he had been brought up; and he went to the synagogue, as his custom was, on the Sabbath day. And he stood up to read; and there was given to him the book of the prophet Isaiah. He opened the book and found the place where it was written: "The Spirit of the Lord is upon me, because he has anointed me to preach good news to the poor. He has sent me to proclaim release to the captives and recovering of sight to the blind, to set at liberty those who are oppressed, to proclaim the acceptable year of the Lord." And he closed

> the book, and gave it back to the attendant, and sat down; and the eyes of all in the synagogue were fixed on him. And he began to say to them, "Today this scripture has been fulfilled in your hearing."
>
> > Luke 4:16-21; RSV

Often Jesus stated that His powers, actions, and activities came from God the Father within Him.

> The words that I say to you I do not speak on my own authority; but the Father who dwells in me does his works. Believe me that I am in the Father and the Father in me; or else believe me for the sake of the works themselves. Truly, truly, I say to you, he who believes in me will also do the works that I do; and greater works than these will he do, because I go to the Father.
>
> > John 14:10-12; RSV

Later, in the garden just before His capture and crucifixion, He would teach that, after He went to the Father, He would send the Spirit of Truth, who would be a comforter to us and teach us all things.

His term for this Spirit in the original Greek is *paraclete*, which means counselor, helper, and comforter, and is considered by Christians to be the Spirit of God, the Spirit of the Lord, that will become our companion.

> I will pray the Father, and he will give you another Counselor, to be with you forever, even the Spirit of truth, whom the world cannot receive, because it neither sees him nor knows him; you know him, for he dwells with you, and will be in you. "I will not leave you desolate; I will come to you. Yet a little while, and the world will see me no more, but you will see me; because I live, you will live also. In that day you will know that I am in my Father, and you in me, and I in you.
>
> > John 14:16-20; RSV

He adds to this, saying,

> The Counselor, the Holy Spirit, whom the Father will
> send in my name, he will teach you all things, and bring
> to your remembrance all that I have said to you.
>
> John 14:26; RSV

Later in this teaching, He added more about this Spirit, explaining that He, Jesus, had much more to say, but it could not yet be absorbed by His followers; the Spirit would guide.

> I have yet many things to say to you, but you cannot bear
> them now. When the Spirit of truth comes, he will guide
> you into all the truth; for he will not speak on his own
> authority, but whatever he hears he will speak, and he will
> declare to you the things that are to come.
>
> John 16:12-13; RSV

The disciple Paul added another view into the nature of our consciousness and the Spirit of the Lord: There is a veil that needs to be removed so that we can bear more knowledge, more guidance from the Spirit.

> To this day whenever Moses is read a veil lies over their
> minds; but when a man turns to the Lord the veil is
> removed. Now the Lord is the Spirit, and where the Spirit
> of the Lord is, there is freedom. And we all, with unveiled
> face, beholding the glory of the Lord, are being changed
> into his likeness from one degree of glory to another; for
> this comes from the Lord who is the Spirit.
>
> 2 Corinthians 3:15-18; RSV

To the woman at the well, Jesus explained that "God is spirit, and those who worship him must worship in spirit and truth." (John 4:24; RSV) To Nicodemus, Jesus taught that not only must we be born of flesh, but we must be born anew of the Spirit.

Truly, truly, I say to you, unless one is born of water and
the Spirit, he cannot enter the kingdom of God. That
which is born of the flesh is flesh, and that which is born
of the Spirit is spirit. Do not marvel that I said to you,
"You must be born anew." The wind blows where it wills,
and you hear the sound of it, but you do not know
whence it comes or whither it goes; so it is with every one
who is born of the Spirit.

John 3:5-8; RSV

When we practice the fruit of the Spirit, it nourishes us in a manner
that gradually changes us from predominantly physical, worldly vibrations and consciousness to more spiritual, godly vibrations and consciousness. As one loves, one unites with love, and as the Scriptures
point out: God is love. (1 John 4:8) As we apply these virtuous fruits in
our thoughts, words, and actions each day, we become one with these
virtues, thus united with the Spirit. Then the Spirit gives the gifts that
strengthen us and that expand our minds and hearts in such a manner
that we become increasingly one with God and companionable to
God—the God of the entire universe and all that is in it. The evangelist
Paul wrote:

It is the Spirit himself bearing witness with our spirit that
we are children of God.

Romans 8:16; RSV

Edgar Cayce's discourses affirm this several times in various ways;
here are two:

Doubt not self, nor self's abilities, for in *doing* does strength
come. Keep that consciousness that answers to self, as face
answers to face in the water, and this will bring the answer in self
as to whether the Spirit of the Creative Forces bears witness with
your *own* spirit.   EC 262-7

Why is God mindful of an individual soul? *Spirit!* For our spirit,

that is a portion of His Spirit, ever bears witness with His Spirit
as to whether we be the children of God or not.   262-115

The Nature of Spirit

Just what is the nature of Spirit?

The word *Spirit* appears at the very beginning of the Bible, in the
second verse of the first chapter of Genesis: "The Spirit of God moved
upon the face of the waters." The actual Hebrew word for *Spirit* used in
this passage is *Ruwach*, which means "wind," as in "the wind of God
moved upon the face of the waters." Wind is an unseen force *behind* a
manifested condition. We see the leaves and branches of a tree move,
and we know that the unseen wind is the cause.

Jesus picked up on this characteristic when He explained to
Nicodemus the nature of the Spirit: "The wind blows where it will, and
you hear the sound of it but do not know from where it comes or to
where it goes; so is everyone who is born of the Spirit." (John 3:8) Now
these words were written in Greek, and the Greek word here for Spirit is
pneuma, which also means wind but has the added connotation of *breath*.
Breath is personal wind; we inhale the Spirit of God and it becomes a
personal spirit within us. This is seen in the second chapter of Genesis
when God breathed the breath of life into humankind and we became
living souls. (Genesis 2:7)

Edgar Cayce also compared God to breath and wind: "God is but as
the breath or the wind in its passing, yet in its passing may quicken . . .
each atom." (EC 1158-5)

Spirit is the life force. In the biblical book of Job, Elihu acknowledges
that the Spirit has given life to us when he says, "the Spirit of God hath
made me." (Job 33:4) God's Spirit gives life to all, including minerals,
plants, and animals. Where there is Spirit, there is life.

In addition to life, the Spirit brings wisdom and understanding. Elihu
stated this in the book of Job: "It is the Spirit in a man, the breath of the
Almighty, that makes him understand." (Job 32:8-9) We also see how the
Spirit brings wisdom when, in the story of the pharaoh who, after being
astonished by Joseph's wisdom, asked his counselors, "Can we find such
a man as this, in whom is the Spirit of God? Since God has shown you

all this, there is none so discreet and wise as you are." (Gen. 41:38–39)

Spirit is the life force and brings enlightenment to our consciousness. Here are three of Edgar Cayce's insights on the Spirit.

> God and the Christ Spirit is Life itself; and the motivating force of the soul is either for that companionship, that association, that development which will make such a soul-body as a fit companion for that Creative Influence manifested in the earth in Him, or it is for separating self from Him.   EC 524-2

> Know . . . an ideal must be beyond the purely material things in life, or in an experience in the earth. For these that are of the earth-earthy rust and corrupt. But those that are founded in the spirit of life and truth take hold upon the very throne of mercy and peace and harmony and justice and long-suffering and brotherly love; for they are *of* God—and thus are everlasting!
> EC 1125-1

> Spirit is life, whether related to the physical functioning of the atomic forces within the system or whether that of the mental being of a body, and these must coordinate in the proper direction one with another, just as much as it is necessary for a physical functioning organ to coordinate with the rest of the system.   EC 2357-1

Let's now study each of the Fruits of the Spirit in an effort to understand them better so that we may apply them in our thinking, speaking, and acting and thereby become one with the Spirit, expanding our hearts and minds for a more soulful life. In this manner we will realize the great potential that God knows is in each of us, even the least among us, as the Bible often phrases it.

4

The Fruit of Love

In spite of all indignant protests to the contrary, the fact remains that love, its problems and its conflicts, is of fundamental importance in human life and, as careful inquiry consistently shows, is of far greater significance than the individual suspects.

Carl Jung; *Two Essays in Analytical Psychology*

The great tragedy of life is not that men perish, but that they cease to love.

Somerset Maugham; *The Summing Up*

To love and be loved is among the highest of human pleasures. The three warmest words to hear and to say are "I love you." Where hate brings contention, strife, faultfinding, and bitterness, love brings patience, understanding, forgiveness, kindness, and joy. Where hate brings destruction and unhappiness, love brings life and happiness.

Saint Paul said that love is "the greatest." Jesus listed it as the top commandment, summing up the works and teachings of all the laws and prophets. More songs are written about love than anything else. But few of us really understand love.

> It is the fate of sensual love to become extinguished when it is satisfied; for it to be able to last, it must . . . be mixed with purely tender components—with such, that is, as are inhibited in their aims.
> Sigmund Freud; *The Letters of Sigmund Freud*

The Science of Love

From a scientific point of view, love is a combination of the forces of evolution and biochemistry.

Evolution's unswerving drive for survival of the species has grabbed onto human bonding because the weaving of pairs of individuals into interdependent couples increases the reproductive success of the parents and the survival rate of their infants.

Evolution has developed a human body that is loaded with powerful chemicals to help ensure the success of human bonding. The "love chemical" is phenylethylamine (PEA). When this is released in the brain of any human, he or she will feel uncontrollably amorous, romantic, and "turned on" by the person who is the object of these feelings. Follow this up with a little oxytocin (often called "the cuddle chemical"), and you have the lovemaking sensations of relaxed satisfaction and attachment. For the relationship to endure, however, endorphins must be released in the brain. If they are, then the love relationship endures.

Evolution's drive—to create human bonding for the greater good of the species—and powerful biochemistry make love one of the strongest forces in human nature.

> The emotion, the ecstasy of love, we all want, but God spare us the responsibility.
> Jessamyn West; *Love is Not What You Think*

The Psychology of Love

The ability to love and express love is dependent upon childhood caregiving. Much research has documented three bonding orientations in children that carry over into adulthood. In psychological terms, the three bonding orientations are (1) secure bonding, (2) ambivalent bonding, and (3) avoidant bonding.

Secure bonding develops when childhood care is consistent and comforting to the child and offers a safe base from which to explore the world. Such children grow into adults that have a secure orientation toward bonding, which results in an orientation that engenders trust, lasting relationships, shared intimacy, and the ability to work out conflicts through compromise.

Ambivalent bonding develops when the childhood care is inconsistent, creating doubts in the child about the caregiver's availability and the safety of the base from which to explore the world. Such children grow up to view themselves poorly and become preoccupied with keeping their romantic partners close at hand and firmly committed.

Avoidant bonding develops when the childhood-care needs are repeatedly rejected or the caregiver is frequently upset or violent. Raised in such an environment, these children develop avoidant patterns. As adults, they will avoid emotional intimacy, looking down upon it or dreading any hints of it.

> This is the worst of life, that love does not give us common sense but is a sure way of losing it. We love people, and we say that we were going to do more for them than friendship, but it makes such fools of us that we do far less, indeed sometimes what we do could be mistaken for the work of hatred.
>
> Rebecca West, quoted in *Rebecca West: Artist and Thinker* by Peter Wolfe

The Philosophy of Love

From a philosophical perspective, love has been categorized into three major types, using the Greek words *eros*, *philia*, and *agape*.

Eros refers to love that is passionate, intense, and sexual, even erotic. However, Plato held that, deep down, eros actually seeks transcendental beauty, but human beauty reminds one of that transcendent beauty.

Philia is fondness and appreciation of the other, beyond self. It is friendship, family loyalty, community ties, love for one's work, and the like. Philia is associated with "brotherly," as in Philadelphia (*phila-delphi*, city of brotherly love).

Agape refers to God's love for His/Her children and to humanity's love for one another. Such love does not seek anything in return for its expression. However, it has an ethical standard and may therefore impartially determine another's warranting love—something we acknowledge today as tough love, meaning a love that calls the other to higher levels of behavior. In the New Testament, written in Greek, many of the "love" statements use the word *agape*.

> One makes mistakes: that is life. But it is never quite a mistake to have loved.
>
> Romain Rolland, *Summer*

The Spirituality of Love

Throughout the Bible, love is most important and powerful. When we think of power, even spiritual power, we rarely think of love. Yet, from Genesis to the Revelation, the Bible indicates that love evokes the highest, most godly of powers and actually is the nature of God. Love brings us closest to our true, divine nature—our angelic nature. Many biblical passages teach that of all the things a person can learn and do in this world, nothing reflects godliness more than love.

The two greatest commandments are found in both the Old and New Testaments. The first:

> You shall love the Lord your God with all your heart, and with all your soul, and with all your mind.
>
> Deuteronomy 6:5 and Matthew 22:37

And the second commandment:

> You shall love your neighbor as yourself.
> > Leviticus 19:18 and Matthew 22:39

The actual Greek word used here is *plesion*, meaning a "close-by person." This expands "neighbor" to include humans within our orb of life.

Perhaps the most quoted love passage in Scripture is the disciple Paul's famous statement in 1 Corinthians 13:13:

> Now abide faith, hope, and love, these three; but the greatest of these is love.

Paul described love beautifully:

> Love is patient, love is kind, and is not jealous; love does not brag and is not arrogant, does not act unbecomingly; it does not seek its own, is not provoked, does not take into account a wrong suffered, does not rejoice in unrighteousness, but rejoices with the truth; bears all things, believes all things, hopes all things, endures all things. Love never fails.
> > 1 Corinthians 4-8

In these passages, the Greek word used for *love* is *agape*, meaning love like God has for His/Her children and creation.

The disciple Peter advised:

> Above all things, keep fervent in your love for one another, because love covers a multitude of sins.
> > 1 Peter 4:8

And John wrote:

> Beloved, let us love one another, for love is from God; and everyone who loves is born of God and knows God. The one who does not love does not know God, for God is love . . . If we love one another, God abides in us, and

His love is perfected in us.

1 John 4:7-12

Jesus spoke of levels of love, identifying the highest love in this often quoted passage:

> Greater love has no man [woman] than this, that a man gives up his [her] life for his friends.
>
> John 15:13; brackets mine

Most have come to understand that Jesus did not mean literal death, rather the giving up of self's desires for another's needs. It is thinking more of what another may need than what self may want. Yet this must not become self-destructive. No one could accuse Jesus of being a door-mat of self-deprecating love. He often radiated a tough love. Those around Him often needed to hear the truth and a clear position on God's ways, not to be pampered. Perhaps the best examples are his discussions with Peter. One instance was when Jesus began to share with his disciples the path that God had laid out for Him to walk:

> he [Jesus] must go to Jerusalem, and suffer many things of the elders and chief priests and scribes, and be killed, and the third day be raised up. Peter took him, and began to rebuke him, saying, "Be it far from you, Lord; this shall never be for you." But Jesus turned, and said to Peter, "Get behind me, Satan; you are a stumbling-block to me for you mind not the things of God but the things of men."
>
> Matthew 16:21-23; brackets mine

For his own sake, Peter needed to realize that his thinking was that akin to Satan's, desiring the ways that seem best to humans over those that are known to be God's ways.

Jesus cared so much for others that he would not let them remain in their darkness or misunderstandings. Yet he never condemned them. Rather, He called their mistakes to mind. He also showed a remarkable sense of their inability to handle the full truth, choosing to be patient: "I have yet many things to say to you, but you cannot bear them now." (John 16:12)

A key passage in the New Testament lays down the foundation upon which all other biblical perspectives on love may be understood. The scene is also fascinating.

Jesus is at the temple in Jerusalem, where pigeons are being sacrificed and the smell and smoke are great. An official scribe working at the temple overheard Jesus answering questions, and he liked Jesus' responses; so he asked the Teacher a very important question. Here is the biblical account:

> One of the scribes came, and heard them questioning together, and knowing that Jesus had answered them well, asked him, "What commandment is the first of all?"
>
> Jesus answered, "The first is, Hear, O Israel, The Lord our God, the Lord is one; and you shall love the Lord your God with all your heart, and with all your soul, and with all your mind, and with all your strength. The second is this; you shall love your neighbor as yourself. There is no other commandment greater than these."
>
> And the scribe said unto him, "Of a truth, Teacher, you have well said that the Lord is one and there is none other but God; and to love him with all the heart, and with all the understanding, and with all the strength, and to love one's neighbor as oneself, is much more than all burnt-offerings and sacrifices."
>
> And when Jesus heard that the scribe answered well, he said unto him, "You are close to the kingdom of God."
>
> Mark 12:28-34; RSV

Notice that Jesus acknowledged the wisdom and understanding that the scribe had gained in his personal spiritual search. Notice also that, although the scribe was standing in the physical world, Jesus said that he was close to the kingdom of God. This reveals that the kingdom of God is not beyond this world and physicality. Heaven may be ap-

proached while incarnate. Additionally, notice that an official of the
temple, in which the practice of animal- and grain-burning were part
of the daily ritual, had come to know that these sacrifices were not what
God sought from his people. God seeks love from us—love toward God
and toward our neighbors.

Keep in mind that those who live with us are our closest neighbors,
though we often take them for granted. These most assuredly should
receive our love.

The Edgar Cayce readings add an interesting perspective to Jesus' use
of the name Israel. They say that the *real* Israel is reflected in the origin
of this name, which is Jacob's seeking so persistently to be blessed by
God that he actually wrestles with an angel of God's until the angel
finally agrees to bless him. Here is that passage. (Notice that Jacob is "by
himself" yet wrestling, which is the indication that he is wrestling *in the
spirit*, with an angel of the Lord.)

> Jacob was by himself; and a man was fighting with him till
> dawn. But when the man saw that he was not able to
> overcome Jacob, he gave him a blow in the hollow part
> of his leg, so that his leg was damaged. And he said to him,
> "Let me go now, for the dawn is near." But Jacob said,
> "I will not let you go till you have given me your
> blessing." Then he said, "What is your name?" And he
> said, "Jacob." And he said, "Your name will no longer be
> Jacob, but Israel: for in your fight with God and with men
> you have overcome."
>
> Then Jacob said, "What is your name?" And he said,
> "What is my name to you?" Then he gave him a blessing.
>
> And Jacob gave that place the name of Peniel, saying,
> I have seen God face to face, and still I am living.
>
> Genesis 32:24-30; BBE

Here's Cayce's explanation of this:

> *This* is the meaning, this should be the understanding to all:
> Those that seek are Israel. "Think not to call yourselves the

promise in Abraham. Know you not that the Lord is able to raise up children of Abraham from the very stones?" So Abraham means *the call;* so Israel means *those who seek.* How obtained the supplanter [this is the literal meaning of the Hebrew name Jacob] the name Israel? He wrestled with the angel, and he was face to face with the seeking to know His way. So it is with us that are called and seek His face; we are the Israel!

262-28 and 5377-1; brackets mine

A New Commandment

A new commandment I give to you, that you love one another; even as I have loved you, that you also love one another.

John 13:34; RSV

By this shall all men know that you are my disciples, if you have love one to another.

John 13:35; RSV

Clearly, Jesus is calling us to come to know love and to live in love. His group will be identifiable by this one characteristic: they express love.

The disciple Paul took up this new way, writing:

Owe no man anything, save to love one another: for he that loves his neighbor has fulfilled the law.

Romans 13:8; RSV

Paul had much to say in his affirming of love's role in the spiritual life, the most famous being this passage:

If I speak with the tongues of men and of angels, but have not love, I am become sounding brass, or a clanging cymbal. And if I have the gift of prophecy, and know all mysteries and all knowledge; and if I have all faith, so as

to remove mountains, but have not love, I am nothing.
And if I bestow all my goods to feed the poor, and if I give
my body to be burned, but have not love, it profits me
nothing. Love suffers long, and is kind; love envies not;
love exalts not itself, is not puffed up, love never fails—
but where there be prophecies, they shall be done away;
where there be tongues, they shall cease; where there be
knowledge, it shall be done away. But now abides faith,
hope, love, these three; and the greatest of these is love.
Follow after love; let all that you do be done in love. My
love be with you all in Christ Jesus. Amen.

Excerpts taken from 1 Corinthians 13-16

It is in one of the letters of the apostle John that we find an important
insight into why love is so important. John tells us that the quintessen-
tial quality of God is *love*. Love is the music of God, the vibration of God,
and the spirit of God.

My loved ones, let us have love for one another because
love is of God, and everyone who has love is a child of God
and has knowledge of God. He who has no love has no
knowledge of God, because God is love. No man has ever
seen God; if we have love for one another, God is in us and
his love is made complete in us. His Spirit, which he has
given us, is the witness that we are in him and he is in us.
And we have seen and had faith in the love, which God
has for us. God is love, and everyone who has love is in
God, and God is in him.

1 John 4:7-16; BBE

God is love, and all who live and express love, live in and express God.
Perhaps the most difficult of the teachings on love is that we are not
only to love our neighbors but also our enemies.

You have heard that it was said, you shall love your
neighbor, and hate your enemy; but I say to you, love

your enemies, and pray for them that persecute you; that you may be sons [and daughters] of your Father who is in heaven: for he makes his sun to rise on the evil and the good, and sends rain on the just and the unjust. For if you love them that love you, what reward have you? Do not even the publicans [tax collectors] the same? And if you salute your brethren only, what do you more than others? Do not even the Gentiles the same? You therefore shall be perfect, as your heavenly Father is perfect.

Matthew 5:43-48, ASV; brackets mine

Perfect? Yes, Jesus wants us to become perfect, as is our Heavenly Father. Paul affirms the *perfecting power* of active love for all in this statement:

Above all these things put on love, which is the bond of perfection.

Colossians 3:14

Jesus expanded on this teaching:

But love your enemies, and do them good, and lend, never despairing; and your reward shall be great, and you shall be sons of the Most High: for he is kind toward the unthankful and evil.

Luke 6:35

If God expresses lovingkindness to the ungrateful and wicked, how can we become companions with God if we cannot do likewise?

A Mystical-Psychic View of Love

To say that love is an exchange of psychic energy is to know life at a deeper level. For example:

The woman who scans the face of her lover anxiously when he is disturbed, and reaches out with a soothing

hand to comfort him, is actually transmitting to him a
healing force within her own nature. She is obeying the
same kind of impulse that directs the heart to pump more
blood to the wounded limb.

Dr. Smiley Blanton, Love or Perish

Edgar Cayce, one of America's greatest seers and psychics, devoted
over two thousand of his more than fourteen thousand "readings" to
teaching spiritual seekers to live, think, speak, and abide in love. Here
are his comments to four different people, obtained while he was attuned to the Universal Consciousness:

> Let the beauty of your joy, in manifesting the light and love as
> shown in the Christ-Spirit, that makes for the new song in your
> heart, keep you in your daily walks of life.
>
> Let others do as they may, but as for you and your house, you
> will love the living God. Know His love is sufficient to keep you.
> No matter what may be the trial, His love abides, and He is not
> unmindful of your prayers.
>
> The beauty of your life rises as a sweet incense before the altar
> of mercy. Yet it is not sacrifice but peace, grace, and mercy that
> we would manifest among the children of men. For God is love.
>
> Keep your paths straight. Know in whom you have believed,
> as well as in what you believe. For the love as passes understand-
> ing can, does, and will make your pathway brighter. Keep in that
> way.   EC 262-116

A mature love requires that we "rightly divine and divide the truth."
Cayce often referred to this teaching, as in this example:

> First, study to show yourself approved unto God, a workman not
> ashamed, rightly divining—or dividing—the words of truth; that
> is, giving proper evaluations to the material, the mental, and the
> spiritual relationships, the economic, the social, the orders of
> things in their proper form. Be not hasty in decisions but know
> that the answers may come from within.   EC 189-3

From his deep trance state, Cayce said that Jesus had a secret prayer that He repeated to himself, "Others, Lord, others." This kept the Father's power that flowed through Jesus on the right track—not glorifying Himself but revealing the Light and Love that flowed through Him—God's love, our Father and Mother's love. Selfless loving is the ideal—giving, caring without expectation of getting something in return.

The Ways of Love

In our personal search for spiritual understanding, nothing will empower and illuminate us more than love. But its ways are subtle and gentle, choosing to work in the background, quietly. Its workshop is our own hearts and minds, its testing grounds our everyday life and everyday relationships. Prayer and meditation can enhance our ability to understand and practice love in daily life. Supplicant prayer, followed by a rising sense of entering into God's presence and abiding there in loving at-onement, will yield our better self. This loving presence will manifest in little things throughout the day—little things that usually only God and our individual soul know.

These loving experiences often leave us humbled but happy and content. Marriage, parenting, friendship, work, and self-esteem will all improve when love is carried in one's heart and mind.

God truly is love. And abiding in God's love is transcending, lifting us beyond our normal perspective. "Seek ye first His kingdom (Love), and all else will be added to you." (Matthew 6:33)

Giving of Ourselves

Of the many activities that we may do to enhance our love, giving is one of the most powerful. In fact, according to Edgar Cayce's reading of the Universal Wisdom, real power only comes through giving. The laws of the universe are simply arranged this way by an all-wise, loving Creator. In a rather involved reading, Cayce explains the dynamics of this arrangement:

> . . . the power comes in giving the expression of the inner self,

letting the soul manifest while letting the personality of self become less and less in its desires, letting His desire be the ruling force. As He gave out, so was the power, the ability, the experience His that He *is*, *was*, and *ever will be* the *concrete* expression of love in the minds, the hearts, the souls of men.

Then, broaden your field of activity. . . . For the more and more that you have many giving praises and thanks for the hope that you create in their minds and their hearts, greater is the experience and the *ability* of expression. For the law, the love holds as He gave; one may cry aloud and long for *self* and yet *never* be heard, but where two or three are gathered in His name there is He in the midst of them. So, as you give out, the power is received.

You may enter into your own closet and there meet your Savior within, but–as given–when you cry for self, and self alone, you close the door, you stand as a shadow before the altar of your god within yourself.

Give, then, in broader fields of activity, in *every* channel where those that are seeking may find; that are wandering, that are lame in body, lame in mind, halt in their manner of expression, that are blind to the beauties in their own household, their own hearts, their own minds. These you may awaken in all your fields. And as you do, greater is your vision–and He will guide you, for He has given His angels charge concerning those that seek to be a channel of blessing to their fellow man; that purge their hearts, their bodies, of every selfish motive and give the Christ–*crucified, glorified*–a place in their stead.   EC 696-3

In this reading Cayce is calling us to broaden our activities of service. He is calling us to give of ourselves, our inner selves, that more power will flow to us as we give to others. He explains that even the Master grew in power as *He* gave out to others. In another of his deep trance readings, Cayce guides us with a little prayer that he says Jesus used during His incarnation:

It is others you must think of, as should every soul: "Others,

> Lord, others—that I may know You the better." This is a part of
> the service of each soul in its sojourn through material forces: to
> think of "Others, Lord," rather than self.   EC 3657-1

> For as individuals do forget themselves and are willing to pour
> out their virtues . . . for the benefit of others, great may be the
> reward. For as you do it unto the least of your fellow man you
> do it unto your Maker, your God.   EC 2310-2

Getting beyond self's interests and concerns by giving love, understanding, and aid to others in their struggles day by day, even taking
upon ourselves some of their burden, enables us to get beyond our
weaknesses and brings great contentment and peace.

> This is Knowledge: that you show yourself approved unto that
> which is set in Him that has shown you the pattern, that has made
> the way straight; that those who seek Him may not be confused,
> that they who love His coming will act as those that are in close
> communion with Him from day to day. This is Knowledge, that
> you love one another, that you show forth in your dealings with
> your fellow man day by day that you care, you understand, you
> are willing to take a portion of the burden of those that are so
> heavily burdened with the cares of life, the cares of the world, the
> deceitfulness of riches; that you are willing to aid those in
> distress, you are willing to feed those that are hungry—not just
> materially. For the world is crying for that Knowledge. It is
> opened to you that have made the choice that you will empty
> yourselves of those little differences that breed hate, contempt;
> and those things that hurt and hurt in your dealings with your
> fellow man. Forgive, if you would be forgiven. That is Knowl-
> edge. Be friendly, if you would have friends. That is Knowledge.
> Be lovely, if you would have the love even of your Father; for He
> is love. This indeed is Knowledge.   EC 262-97

Lovingly giving to those we meet, without thought of reward or glory,
opens us to more inflow of love from God:

... in the heart love finds its way. Love is conceived as of God, as all pleasant, as all giving; given in that great expression: "God so loved the world as to give His only begotten son; that through Him we might have eternal life."

Yet the other side, or the reverse of love, is suffering, hate, malice, injustice.   EC 281-51

The readings explain:

There needs to be a better coordination between the physical, mental and spiritual being . . . in the giving you possess the power, the strength, the healing, the ministration, the giving of all those forces and influences that are of a creative nature.
                                                                         EC 2164-1

Few activities make humans as happy as giving, for few activities are as expressive of God and God's way.

For the sun of light may shine in the hearts of many by the turn of the hand of the entity in giving to others the power, the ability to give of themselves. For only that you give may you take with you into eternity.   EC 1438-1

Through the giving, through the action, there comes the knowledge of the power being manifest, and those great truths resound, redound, through the life, through the whole being of the entity, see? Beautiful!   EC 900-151

In the giving you possess the power, the strength, the healing.
                                                                         EC 2164-1

The Role of the Spirit in Our Hearts and Minds

In the passages that Cayce's readings so often recommended, John 14 through 17, Jesus related that, after His ascension, He would send the Spirit to comfort and help humankind in every way. He called the Spirit the "comforter" and encouraged us to seek this Spirit's presence within our hearts and minds.

Paul picked up on this, identifying the Spirit as an important source of love:

> The love of God has been shed abroad in our hearts through the Holy Spirit which was given to us.
>
> Romans 5:5; ASV

Paul was so filled with the love of God that comes through the Holy Spirit that, even in the midst of hard times, he wrote:

> Who shall separate us from the love of Christ? Shall tribulation, or anguish, or persecution, or famine, or nakedness, or peril, or sword? Even as it is written: For your sake we are killed all the daylong. We were accounted as sheep for the slaughter. No, in all these things we are more than conquerors through him that loved us. For I am persuaded that neither death, nor life, nor angels, nor principalities, nor things present, nor things to come, nor powers, nor height, nor depth, nor any other creature, shall be able to separate us from the love of God.
>
> Romans 8:35-39; ASV

Like Paul, Edgar Cayce understood how difficult life could be. He encouraged us not to kick against the thorns of life but to engage love, for this will bring us closer to a happier, more creative life.

> Kick not against the pricks but *love* good, love honor, love patience. For divine love may bring the knowledge, the understanding, the wisdom for the activities to bring the self in accord with Creative Forces.   EC 1215-4

Edgar Cayce's readings strongly affirm the importance of love—active love—in our daily lives:

Know in Whom you believe as well as in what you believe. Know the source of your knowledge and you may know the end thereof. Know the laws—or the love; for the law of God is *love* of God, and is not a hardship. For the law as man's law kills, but the love of the law as of God makes alive—every one. And your Lord, your God, is God of the living. Make your life and your love of your fellow man a living thing in your experience day by day. Smile oft. Speak gently. Be kind.   EC 262-109

Cayce's discourses call on us to "keep the fires of love burning in your hearts day by day, for the love of God is manifested in the earth through those that are just kind one to another." (EC 281-17) Following on the idea that God's Spirit brings life and light to us, Cayce notes that "love is wisdom, as love is God." (EC 262-108) Since God is love, it is wise to live lovingly. But Cayce adds a little caveat to this approach: Be careful not to be loving for selfish interests.

In seeking, let it be not for self, rather that there may come in your experience the greater channel of blessing for your friend— yea, your enemy, for the love of God constrains you that you faint not by the way. Condemn not and you will not be condemned. Love not and you will not be loved. But He that would show forth the love that the Father hath bestowed upon you will be *lovely* to every soul!   EC 705-1

Nature—God's Expression of Love

Cayce's readings associate Nature with God, that the beauty and wonder of Nature are loving gifts from God to us. In Nature we can feel God's expression of life.

Have more and know more of Nature and of God's outdoors, rather than man's. See nature not "in the rough," then; rather in the expressions of Life! For each blade of grass, each blossom, each tree, each crag, each mountain, each river, each lake is as a gift from the Creative Forces in man's experience that he may

know more of the love of God. And as a soul, as a developing
body then sees in the creatures, in the various kingdoms as *they*
care for their young, as they are selective in their mating, as they
are mindful of the influences and the environs, learn from these
Nature's lessons or God's expression to the children of men; that
He indeed is in His holy temple and is *mindful* of man's estate—
if *man* minds the *laws* of nature, of God. For love is law, love is
God.   EC 1248-1

Law and Love

Notice that Cayce associates love with law. This is not a feature normally associated with love. According to Cayce, love is not unstructured
or unbounded giving and caring—it must coexist within the context of
truth. Today we use the term "tough love" to describe this. To Cayce, it
was the balance of love with truth, for one without the other creates an
imbalance.

You will come to that realization, as was expressed in Him, that
as you abide in truth and love, truth and love abide in you,
bringing into your experience more and more harmonious
forces, bringing peace that takes away fear, doubt from your
experience.   EC 2073-2

In a discourse about the greatness of the United States way of life,
Cayce stated:

Freedom means rather the individuals working in cooperation
according to the dictates of their conscience as to the *manner* of
worship, but the *worship itself* of Truth, Life, Love, Brotherly
Love, and Kindness! And these are the basis of this land; and its
union of strength lies in *keeping* such as the motivative forces in
the lives and hearts and minds of those as they labor one with
another.   EC 1151-12

Our love includes truth: "Life is truth. Truth is love. Love is God.

God is life." (EC 5733-1)

This next Cayce discourse encourages us to seek an inner connection with God, in our hearts and minds. This will bring the Spirit's reaction into our daily experiences and the experiences of those around us, whom we are called to love.

> His promises are true: "I will not leave you comfortless, but will come and abide with you."
>
> In such experiences in self, then, may there be added to the lesson on Love that which will awaken in the hearts, the souls, the minds of others that desire to know *His* ways better.
>
> Each has been chosen as a channel, and each in its own way, and not alone of self, but manifesting life through love will bring the Spirit's reaction in the daily experiences of every soul. For, they are one—*all* believe, all have heard. Then, let them that have eyes see, and ears hear, what the Spirit says unto them in such meditation in the *inner* self.
>
> For, from the abundance of the heart the mouth speaks; and the love of the Father through the Son constrains all, if each will be less selfish, less self-centered, more desirous of showing forth *His* love, His abundant mercy, His peace, His harmony, that comes from being quiet in the Lord, being joyous in service, being happy in whatsoever state you find self; knowing that he whom the Lord loves, him does He call into service.
>
> EC 262-46

Our service is to love one another—both the easy to love and the not so easy. In so doing, we become an expression, a channel of God's love. As we continue with this, we become one with God. His love and our love are the same.

5

The Fruit of Forgiveness

Forgiveness Implies Sin and Transgression

Since forgiveness implies wrongdoing, even to the level of sin, it is helpful to understand a little more about sin, evil, and transgression. How did all of this begin? How has it proceeded? And where is it ultimately headed? Let's look at some of the answers to these questions.

Original Sin

In the Western world, the first great sin, or at least the first transgression, was Eve and Adam's eating of the fruit of a forbidden and strangely named tree: Tree of the Knowledge of Good and Evil. We may assume that, by tasting evil, humans came to know evil, something God wanted to avoid. However, once having partaken of this fruit, many changes followed. The most devastating was the loss of direct companionship with the Creator. The biblical story indicates that direct companionship was lost because humans became self-conscious of being in the presence of the All-Knowing.

This costly sin was then quickly followed by Cain's jealousy-driven murder of his brother, which resulted in the need to go further away from God's presence.

The Seven Deadly Sins

Eve and Adam's lust for the forbidden fruit and Cain's jealousy of his brother are among the "Seven Deadly Sins." Pope Gregory the Great first formally identified the Seven Deadly Sins in the 6th Century AD (note that the sin of envy also includes jealousy):

1. Envy
2. Lust
3. Pride
4. Wrath
5. Sloth
6. Gluttony
7. Greed.

In his classic *Divine Comedy*, Dante identified these seven deadly sins and turned them into levels in Hell and Purgatory. He placed Cain among the leaders of the last level of Hell. The *Divine Comedy* distinguishes those in Hell from those in Purgatory: in Hell, humans justify their sins; in Purgatory, they seek to change the urge within them that led to their sins. Each time Dante purged himself of a sin, his body became lighter, less weighed down by the sin, ultimately allowing him to enter the heavens. This leads us to consider the "Seven Virtues" that counterbalance the seven deadly sins.

The Seven Virtues

The corresponding virtues, if applied in one's life, can subdue the influence of the seven deadly sins:

1. Faith
2. Hope
3. Charity
4. Fortitude
5. Justice
6. Prudence
7. Temperance

When considering sin, one has to address the Ten Commandments, given by God through Moses on the Mount. To break one of these commandments is to break a covenant with God. In fact, the commandments are often referred to as the covenant: "If you keep these commandments, then I will be your God." In the Mosaic tradition, these are the Ten Commandments:

1. I am the Lord your God.
2. Have no other gods before me and make no images or idols.
3. Do not misuse my name.
4. Keep holy the Sabbath.
5. Honor your parents.
6. Do not kill.
7. Do not commit adultery.
8. Do not steal.
9. Do not bear false witness.
10. Do not covet your neighbor's spouse or property.

Catholic and Lutheran traditions merge the first two commandments into one and separate the last one into two separate commandments. Some Protestant traditions (except Lutheran) do not use the first commandment, listed above, and separate the second into two commandments.

In one fortuitous exchange in the Bible, we come to the knowledge that, for all intents and purposes, the Ten Commandments may be distilled down to two and that these two are apparently the sum of "all of the laws and the prophets." For, when asked what the two greatest commandments are, Jesus answered:

> You shall love the Lord your God with all your heart, and
> with all your soul, and with all your mind. This is the great
> and first commandment. And a second is like it; you shall
> love your neighbor as yourself. On these two command-
> ments depend all the law and the prophets.
>
> Matthew 22:37

In Jesus' parables, he added to our list of sins a new and uncomfort-
able one: sins of *omission*. These are sins that result from our not doing
anything! This troubling concept first appears in Matthew:

> When the Son of man comes in his glory, and all the
> angels with him, then he will sit on his glorious throne.
> Before him will be gathered all the nations, and he will
> separate them one from another as a shepherd separates
> the sheep from the goats, and he will place the sheep at
> his right hand, but the goats at the left. Then the King will
> say to those at his right hand, "Come, O blessed of my
> Father, inherit the kingdom prepared for you from the
> foundation of the world; for I was hungry and you gave
> me food, I was thirsty and you gave me drink, I was a
> stranger and you welcomed me, I was naked and you
> clothed me, I was sick and you visited me, I was in prison
> and you came to me." Then the righteous will answer
> him, "Lord, when did we see you hungry and feed you,
> or thirsty and give you drink? And when did we see you
> a stranger and welcome you, or naked and clothe you?
> And when did we see you sick or in prison and visit you?"
> And the King will answer them, "Truly, I say to you, as
> you did it to one of the least of these my brethren, you did
> it to me." Then he will say to those at his left hand,
> "Depart from me, you cursed, into the eternal fire
> prepared for the devil and his angels; for I was hungry and
> you gave me no food, I was thirsty and you gave me no
> drink, I was a stranger and you did not welcome me,
> naked and you did not clothe me, sick and in prison and

you did not visit me." Then they also will answer, "Lord,
when did we see you hungry or thirsty or a stranger or
naked or sick or in prison, and did not minister to you?"
Then he will answer them, "Truly, I say to you, as you did
it not to one of the least of these, you did it not to me."
And they will go away into eternal punishment, but the
righteous into eternal life.

Matthew 25:31-46

This approach to sin harkens back to Cain's classic question to God,
"Am I my brother's keeper?" It also touches Jesus' comment that the
second greatest commandment is like the first— Love your neighbor as
yourself—which is often stated as the Golden Rule: Do to others as you
would have them do to you. Sins of omission result from ignoring or
not caring about the needs of our sisters and brothers.

This leads us to the Eastern world's view of sin, which, for the most
part, is viewed as being the result of ignorance. It is assumed that if one
truly knew the karma of one's sins, or transgressions, one would never
commit them. Therefore, at the root of all sin is *ignorance*. The way to
counter sin—all sin—is to become enlightened about the effects of
wrongdoing on one's psyche and life (not to mention one's future in-
carnations).

The roots of evil and sin have been of interest since the dawn of
human activity. In an attempt to find the single most causal urge for
evil, humans have named several sources. One often hears the quotation from 1 Timothy 6:10, "The love of money is the root of all evils."
Here is the full text of this passage:

There is great gain in godliness with contentment; for we
brought nothing into the world, and we cannot take
anything out of the world; but if we have food and
clothing, with these we shall be content. But those who
desire to be rich fall into temptation, into a snare, into
many senseless and hurtful desires that plunge men into
ruin and destruction. *For the love of money is the root of all
evils*, it is through this craving that some have wandered

away from the faith and pierced their hearts with many pangs. But as for you, man of God, shun all this; aim at righteousness, godliness, faith, love, steadfastness, gentleness. Fight the good fight of the faith; take hold of the eternal life to which you were called.

1 Timothy 6:6-12; italics mine

Certainly, humanity's greed-driven activities have resulted in many sinful acts. However, in the Bible's story of Eve giving the forbidden apple to Adam, many have tainted woman with original sin. Add to this the biblical passage indicating that the Sons of God fell from grace because of their lust for women: "The sons of God saw that the daughters of men were fair; and they took them wives of all that they chose." (Genesis 6:2) And then add the more modern saying—When all else fails, the Devil sends a woman—and we have the strange association of woman with evil.

However, this view overlooks the implications of Genesis 3:15 when God stated that woman's "seed" will subdue the influence of the serpent's evil. In this passage God said, "I will put enmity between you [the serpent] and the woman, and between your seed and her seed; he [her seed] shall bruise your head, and you shall bruise his heel." (Brackets mine.) Throughout the Bible we find women playing key roles in the struggle to keep good and godliness alive amid evil and earthiness. In Genesis we find,

There were twins in her womb [Rebekah's]. And the first [newborn] came forth red all over, like a hairy garment; and they called his name Esau. And after that came forth his brother, and his hand had hold on Esau's heel; and his name was called Jacob . . .

When the boys grew up, Esau was a skilful hunter, a man of the field; and Jacob was a quiet man, dwelling in tents. Now Isaac loved Esau, because he did eat of his venison, and Rebekah loved Jacob . . .

Genesis 25:24-28; brackets mine

Rebecca intuitively sensed it was God's will that Jacob rather than Esau become the leader of the people, so she arranged for her husband, who favored Esau, to mistakenly give his blessing to Jacob rather than to Esau. To add to this, Esau did not care about his first-born birthright to lead the people and carry on God's work, so he sold his birthright to Jacob for a bowl of Jacob's pottage. (Genesis 25:30-34)

Another biblical woman who saved the seekers and got them back home was Esther. Risking her own life, she convinced her husband, the Persian king, to allow her people, the captured Israelites in Babylon, to return to their homeland and rebuild their temple.

But the archetype of woman's role in the redemption and illumination of all is found in the Revelation. In chapter twelve, the disciple John had a vision in which he saw a divine female in the sky. She is standing on the moon, clothed in the sun, with twelve stars above her head. What's more, she is pregnant with the one who will be victorious over evil and bring the whole world into an eternal era of peace and goodness—the Redeemer of the world. All the forces of heaven, including the archangel Michael and his angels, protect her and help her to safely deliver the divine child.

In a fascinating twist on the whole story of the origin and nature of sin, mystic seer Edgar Cayce narrowed it all down to "the only sin is self." Self-centeredness and selfishness are at the root of all evil. Furthermore, he states that the first sin was not in the Garden but in the heavens, long before the Garden. It was a rebellion that began among the angels in heaven. This touches on the legend of the Fallen Angels, who were led by one who truly could be called the first sinner, Lucifer.

Initially, Lucifer, as his name implies ("light bearer"), was one of the most beautiful angels among the two great companies of angels created by God, the Seraphim (Isaiah 6:2) and Cherubim (Genesis 3:24). He was identified with the morning star, Venus. However, he became enamored with himself and began to aspire to be greater than God, a desire that ultimately led to his downfall. Lucifer's fall from power is addressed in the book of Isaiah:

> How you are fallen from heaven, day-star, son of the morning [Venus]! How you are cut down to the ground,

who laid the nations low! You said in your heart, I will
ascend into heaven, I will exalt my throne above the stars
of God; and I will sit on the mountain of congregation,
in the uttermost parts of the north; I will ascend above the
heights of the clouds; I will make myself like the Most
High. Yet you shall be brought down to Sheol [Hell], to
the uttermost parts of the pit. Those who see you shall
gaze at you, they shall consider you, saying, "Is this the
man who made the earth to tremble, who shook kingdoms; who made the world as a wilderness, and over-
threw the cities of it; who didn't let loose his prisoners to
their home?"

Isaiah 14:12-17; brackets mine

Lucifer's rebellion began in the spirit, before the descent of spirit into
flesh or the children of God into physical bodies. As Lucifer was called
the morning star, so were all the children of God who began to descend
from Heaven into the Earth, recorded in the Book of Job, 38:7: "The
morning stars sang together, and all the sons of God shouted for joy."
Most important in this ancient story is that even this original evil influence is redeemed in the last book of the Bible, the Revelation: "Even as
I myself have received power from my Father; I will give him [who
overcomes] the morning star." In the final chapter of the Revelation,
Jesus even identified himself as "the root and offspring of David, the
bright morning star." (Rev. 22:16) This appears to indicate the redemption of the fallen star, the fallen angel, and all those other morning stars
that sang together in the beginning.

Edgar Cayce's mystical discourses on these matters add some interesting perspectives. Here is a paraphrasing of one of his commentaries:

We must know from whence we came; how, why; and whither
we go – and why. The Spirit of God moved and matter came into
being to provide an opportunity for God's companions, God's
sons and daughters. As they used their wills to pursue self-
indulgence, self-glorification, they began to war against one
another, *before* they even entered matter! The spirit contained

the influences and vibrations of selfish motives, which subsequently came into matter, into earth, into the body. That which was spirit now moved to make rebellion. The Spirit of God was now opposed by the spirit of self. This becomes self-evident when we look about us in our own experience day by day. They that have the Spirit of God have the Spirit of Truth, have the Spirit of Christ, have the Spirit of Construction. They that have the spirit of rebellion have the spirit of hate, the spirit of confusion; and seek self-glory rather than peace, harmony and understanding.

Thus as has been indicated, Spirit pushed into matter and became what we see in our three-dimensional world as the kingdoms of the earth (the mineral, the vegetable, the animal). That which bears witness is the Spirit of Truth, the Spirit of Light. For He said, "Let there be light; and there was light." Then indeed there is no power that *emanates* that is not from God.

Then, you ask, what is this spirit of rebellion, what is this spirit of hate? What is this spirit of self-indulgence? What is this spirit that makes men afraid? *Selfishness!* Allowed, yes; it has been allowed by the Creator, the Father. For, as given, He has not willed that the souls should perish but that we each should know the truth – and the truth will make us free. Of what? Selfishness! Then we should each know that the sin which lies at our door [as stated in Genesis 4:7] is ever the sin of selfishness, self-glory, self-honor.   EC 262-114; brackets mine

As we can see, Cayce picked up on many of the key elements of the ancient spiritual legends and biblical stories addressing the origin and nature of sin.

If we take another look at the Seven Deadly Sins, we can see that self and selfishness are at the root of each: envy, lust, pride, wrath, sloth, gluttony, and greed. The counterbalancing influence to these is loving God and others, because such love causes us to reach beyond our self-interests, self-gratifications, and self-exaltations. Truly loving and caring about another's welfare requires us to get beyond our own needs and wants. Truly loving God, the infinite Creator of the universe, requires us to reach beyond our finite, individual awareness—expanding our heart and mind into the greater dimensions of awareness and purpose.

As we narrow our attention upon ourselves, we shrink and become heavy and alone. As we open our attention to those around us and the great, infinite forces of life and creativity, we expand, rise—light and free—and become a part of the greater community of life.

6

The Fruit of Mercy

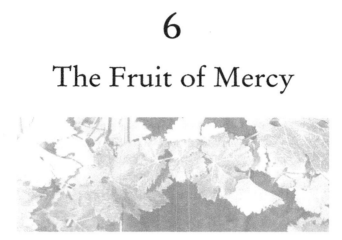

God's Patience and Mercy

One of the earliest examples of God's mercy is found in Genesis, chapter eighteen, when the angels of the Lord were sent to investigate Sodom and Gomorrah. The scene begins with Abraham sitting in the doorway of his tent. He sees the Lord coming in the form of three "men," who are widely interpreted as three *angels* of the Lord manifesting in human form. Here is that opening scene and Abraham's request.

> Now the Lord came to him [Abraham] by the holy tree of Mamre, when he was seated in the doorway of his tent in the middle of the day. And lifting up his eyes, he saw three [angels in the form of] men before him; and seeing them, he went quickly to them from the door of the tent, and went down on his face to the earth; and said, "My

> Lord, if now I have grace in your eyes, do not go away
> from your servant."
>
> Genesis 18:1-3, BBE; brackets mine

These three angels replied by first prophesying the birth of a child to Sarah, the wife of Abraham, even though she was ninety years old. Then, as the angels were departing to Sodom and Gomorrah, the Lord paused to consider sharing his plans with Abraham. The three angels explained that cries from earth over the horrors occurring in Sodom and Gomorrah had brought the Lord to investigate. The three angels departed, but Abraham remained in contact with the Lord, and the following discussion ensued:

> Will you let destruction come on the upright with the
> sinners? If by chance there are fifty upright men in the
> town, will you give the place to destruction and not have
> mercy on it because of the fifty upright men? Let such a
> thing be far from you, to put the upright to death with
> the sinner; will not the judge of all the earth do right?
> And the Lord said, "If there are fifty upright men in the
> town, I will have mercy on it because of them." And
> Abraham answering said, "Truly, I who am only dust,
> have undertaken to put my thoughts before the Lord: If
> by chance there are five less than fifty upright men, will
> you give up all the town to destruction because of these
> five?" And he said, "I will not give it to destruction if
> there are forty-five." And again he said to him, "By
> chance there may be forty there." And he said, "I will not
> do it if there are forty." And he said, "Let not the Lord
> be angry with me if I say, 'What if there are thirty there?'"
> And he said, "I will not do it if there are thirty." And he
> said, "See now, I have undertaken to put my thoughts
> before the Lord: what if there are twenty there?" And he
> said, "I will have mercy because of the twenty." And he
> said, "O let not the Lord be angry and I will say only one
> word more: by chance there may be ten there." And he

said, "I will have mercy because of the ten." And the
Lord went on his way when his talk with Abraham was
ended, and Abraham went back to his place.

Genesis 18:23-33; BBE

Mercy and the Ten Commandments

In this story we see the patience and mercy of the Lord and His
willingness to consider the judgment and considerations of human beings like Abraham.

This next significant statement of mercy occurred during the giving
of the Ten Commandments to Moses. After giving the first and second
commandments, God made this statement to Moses, and through Moses
to us:

And I will have mercy through a thousand generations
on those who have love for me and keep my laws.

Exodus 20:6; BBE

In giving the Ten Commandments, which are the Covenant, the Lord
spoke of *mercy—generations* of mercy!

The Mercy Seat

The next example is also with Moses. God instructed Moses, and
through Moses to humanity, to build a tabernacle so He could be among
His people, even meet them face to face. This becomes the first temple
after the seekers leave Egypt's stone temples. The new temple is por-
table, made with curtains and poles, and traveled with the people. It was
divided into three main areas: the courtyard, the Holy Place, and the
Holy of Holies, which contained the Ark of the Covenant. The Ark was
basically a chest made of acacia wood overlaid with gold. As God guided
Moses and the builders of the new temple, He described a feature that
would be placed on top of the Ark of the Covenant: the Mercy Seat. And
it is "above" this seat and between two statues of Cherub angels that
God promised, "I will come face to face with you." (Exodus 30:6; BBE)

> And when Moses went into the tent of meeting to speak
> with the Lord, he heard the voice speaking to him from
> above the mercy seat that was upon the ark of the
> testimony, from between the two cherubim; and it spoke
> to him.
>
> Numbers 7:89; RSV

Clearly, Mercy is the seat of the throne of God when He meets with us face to face. And rather than two Seraphim angels, God selects two Cherubim. Seraphim are defined as Beings of Fire and are concerned with keeping Divinity in perfect order. They are intense, keen, and tireless in dispelling evil and protecting God's Throne—not exactly forces of mercy. On the other hand, the name Cherubim has a connotation akin to the English words *benevolent blessings*. God directed the builders to construct the Mercy Seat in such a manner as to integrate a cherub on one end of the lid and another on the other end of the lid, as from one piece of wood. Thus the Mercy Seat included these benevolent blessings.

The Hebrew word used at that time for *Mercy Seat* was *kapporeth*, which means "lid" but is derived from the word *kippur*, which means "atonement"! In Middle English (c. 1100 and c. 1500) atonement meant "to be at one," with the connotation that this is achieved by making up for one's incompatible mistakes. In the New Testament, the disciple Paul used the Greek word *hilasterion*, which literally means "place of propitiation," or the place where one atones for sin or wrongdoing. The High Priest sprinkled the blood of atonement on the Mercy Seat seven times on the Day of Atonement—Yom Kippur—a day set aside for fasting, depriving oneself of pleasures, and repenting from the sins of the previous year. It was observed on the tenth day of the seventh month—Tishri—portions of September and October on the Gregorian calendar.

The Temple is Within Us

This temple and its features physically represent the temple of the body, which is the true temple of the living God. The disciple Paul expresses this so well:

> Christ did not go into a holy place that had been made by men's hands as the copy of the true one; but he went into heaven itself, and now takes his place before the face of God for us.
>
> Hebrews 9:24; BBE

Today our temple and the place where God meets with us face to face is in our hearts and minds. Here, in silence and prayerfulness, we meet. "Be still, and know that I am God." (Psalm 46:11; RSV)

"I Seek Mercy, not Sacrifice"

As we move into the New Testament, we also find mercy among the highest fruits of the Spirit. Jesus directed everyone, "Go and learn what this means, 'I desire mercy, and not sacrifice.' For I came not to call the righteous, but sinners." (Matthew 9:13; RSV) God and God's incarnation came to call sinners to redemption and resurrection. The means to this redemption is to show mercy to others who have made mistakes with free will, as Jesus taught in his Sermon on the Mount: "Blessed are the merciful, for they shall obtain mercy." (Matthew 5:7; RSV)

In His parables, one of his favorite ways of teaching, Jesus revealed how important it is for us to show mercy to others because our heavenly Father has shown mercy to us. Here's that parable.

> A lawyer stood up to put him to the test, saying, "Teacher, what shall I do to inherit eternal life?"
>
> He said to him, "What is written in the law? How do you read?"
>
> And he answered, "You shall love the Lord your God with all your heart, and with all your soul, and with all your strength, and with all your mind; and your neighbor as yourself."
>
> And he said to him, "You have answered right; do this, and you will live."
>
> But he, desiring to justify himself, said to Jesus, "And who is my neighbor?"

Jesus replied, "A man was going down from Jerusalem to Jericho, and he fell among robbers, who stripped him and beat him, and departed, leaving him half dead. Now by chance a priest was going down that road; and when he saw him he passed by on the other side. So likewise a Levite, when he came to the place and saw him, passed by on the other side. But a Samaritan, as he journeyed, came to where he was; and when he saw him, he had compassion, and went to him and bound up his wounds, pouring on oil and wine; then he set him on his own beast and brought him to an inn, and took care of him. And the next day he took out two denarii and gave them to the innkeeper, saying, `Take care of him; and whatever more you spend, I will repay you when I come back.' Which of these three, do you think, proved neighbor to the man who fell among the robbers?"

He said, "The one who showed mercy on him."

And Jesus said to him, "Go and do likewise."

Luke 10:25-37; RSV

The apostle James wrote in his Epistle:

The wisdom from above is first pure, then peaceable, gentle, open to reason, full of mercy and good fruits, without uncertainty or insincerity.

James 3:17; RSV

Heavenly wisdom is "full of mercy," because there are few who have not misused free will on occasion. Therefore, mercy is paramount if souls are to reunite with their destiny and eternal life with their Creator. All must show mercy, because the law is perfect: As you sow, so shall you reap. Sow mercy, and you will receive mercy.

The apostle Peter wrote:

Once you were not a people but now you are God's people; once you had not received mercy but

> now you have received mercy.
>
> > 1 Peter 2:10; RSV

In return we are to show mercy to others.
Edgar Cayce taught:

> Put your trust, your understanding, your self, into the hands of
> the *merciful* Father. And as you would have *mercy* from Him,
> *show* mercy to those you contact day by day.   EC 792-1

> Mercy ever, then—not mere sacrifice—Mercy, Lord, for all.
> > EC 3155-1

> Have you found ever that to "get even" with anyone made you
> happy? To forgive them is divine and brings happiness to all.
> *These* things *sow* in the lives, in the hearts, in the minds of others.
> "Grace and mercy, Lord, not sacrifice—nor judgment."
> > EC 262-109

Mercy and Justice

Just as we found with love and truth, so we find how mercy is balanced with justice. Jesus chastised the Pharisees for overlooking the important qualities of a good soul:

> Woe to you, scribes and Pharisees, hypocrites! For you
> tithe mint and dill and cumin, and have neglected the
> weightier matters of the law, justice and mercy and faith;
> these you ought to have done, without neglecting the
> others.
> > Matthew 23:22; RSV

Justice is balanced with mercy, but mercy is paramount. The apostle James wrote:

> For judgment is without mercy to one who has shown no

mercy; yet mercy triumphs over judgment.

James 2:13; RSV

Cayce also balanced mercy with justice:

> From Him we may in mercy find mercy, as we show mercy,
> patience, truth, justice, loving-kindness, to our fellow man. For,
> "As you do it unto these, my brethren, you do it unto me."
>
> EC 262-65

> Let mercy and justice direct you, that the peace which passes all
> understanding may be yours in the consciousness of the Christ-
> Presence.   EC 5758-1

> Love mercy and justice, eschew evil; and keep your heart
> *singing* all the while. For the joy of the service in the love of the
> Lord makes the heart glad.   EC 262-116

7

The Fruit of Patience

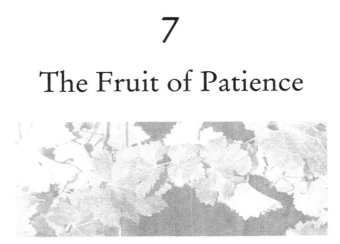

Patience as a Dimension of Consciousness

Edgar Cayce has a strange and fascinating perspective on patience. To him, patience is not just a virtue but another *dimension*. "Time, space, and patience are those channels through which man as a finite mind may become aware of the infinite," he explained. (EC 3161–1) But then, in the same reading, he goes on to say, "There is no time, no space, when patience becomes manifested in love." He explains, "Love un-bounded is patience. Love manifested is patience." (EC 262–24)

When patience becomes an *active* principle in our lives, we rise above the boundaries of time and space. Our finite mind and our human side hold us in the dimensions of time and space, but we have access to our infinite mind, our Christ–like side, which can and will lift us beyond time and space.

Self in the physical grows weary, because you are only human, because you are finite; you have a beginning, you have an end of your patience, your love, your hope, your fear, your desire. But when these problems arise know you cannot walk the whole way alone, but He has promised in the Christ-Consciousness to give you strength, to give you life and that more abundant.

EC 3161-1

In patience run the race that is set before you, looking to Him, the author, the giver of light, truth, and immortality. That should be the central theme in every individual.   EC 262-24

Patience is not passive endurance and submissiveness. It is active, transforming, and filled with the power of God *in action*. "Taking or enduring hardships, or censure, or idiosyncrasies of others, is not necessarily patience at all" (EC 262–24). "Patience is active rather than passive" (EC 262–26). In one of his wonderful twists, Cayce asks us to consider the patience of God's relationship with man. How has God manifested His/Her patience with us? Has He taken away free will? Has He crushed evildoers? Banned non–believers? Cayce noted, "God is God of those who hate Him as well as of those who love Him. He is patient, He is kind, He is merciful" (254–115). Again, Cayce expresses an active quality to patience:

Love unbounded is patience. Love manifested is patience . . . Remove self far from criticisms or fault-findings in others, and there comes then patience in word, deed, and act. EC 262-24

Actively trying to resist finding fault or criticizing others is patience. Actively trying to manifest love, when it hurts, is patience.

Further, "Not in submissiveness alone, but in righteous wrath serve you the living God. Be *mad*, but sin not!" (EC 262–24) Here, William Shakespeare's suggestion that we judge the *act*, not the *actor*, is the better course to take. In this way we may condemn the actions, the words, but withhold condemning the soul that committed them.

Patience requires that we loosen the hold of our finite mind and human side upon us and open ourselves to our infinite mind, the Christ-Consciousness, and our spiritual, godlike side. We should actively run the race set before us—loving, not condemning, those around us and walking the daily path *with* God. When we do this, we live in another dimension, one beyond the limitations of time and space—a path that is eternal and filled with peace that passes all understanding.

Jesus taught, "In your patience possess ye your souls." (Luke 21:19; KJV)

Our soul is immortal. We are more than human. We are godlings of the Infinite, Omnipotent, and Omnipresent God, made in His/Her image. We need to begin using our godly faculties more frequently to become who we ultimately are: companions to and co-creators with God. Active patience in our daily lives is a fruit that gives birth to the Spirit latent within us.

Here's a parable from Jesus:

> And when a great crowd came together and people from town after town came to him, he said in a parable:
>
> "A sower went out to sow his seed; and as he sowed, some fell along the path, and was trodden under foot, and the birds of the air devoured it.
>
> "And some fell on the rock; and as it grew up, it withered away, because it had no moisture.
>
> "And some fell among thorns; and the thorns grew with it and choked it.
>
> "And some fell into good soil and grew, and yielded a hundredfold." As he said this, he called out, "He who has ears to hear, let him hear."
>
> And when his disciples asked him what this parable meant, he said, "To you it has been given to know the secrets of the kingdom of God; but for others they are in parables, so that seeing they may not see, and hearing they may not understand.
>
> "Now the parable is this: The seed is the word of God.
>
> "The ones along the path are those who have heard; then the devil comes and takes away the word from their

hearts, that they may not believe and be saved.

"And the ones on the rock are those who, when they hear the word, receive it with joy; but these have no root, they believe for a while and in time of temptation fall away.

"And as for what fell among the thorns, they are those who hear, but as they go on their way they are choked by the cares and riches and pleasures of life, and their fruit does not mature.

"And as for that in the good soil, they are those who, hearing the word, hold it fast in an honest and good heart, and bring forth fruit with patience."

Luke 8:4-15; RSV

Patience is a most powerful and important fruit of the Spirit. It changes us. It lifts us to new levels of love, faith, and strength.

The disciple Paul wrote,

Rejoice in hope of the glory of God. And not only *so*, but we glory in tribulations also: knowing that tribulation works patience; And patience, experience; and experience, hope: And hope makes not ashamed; because the love of God is shed abroad in our hearts by the Holy Ghost which is given unto us.

Romans 5:2-5; KJV

Now Paul sees a formula: trials build patience, patience builds experience, and experience builds hope. As we handle life's challenges and disappointments in active, faithful patience, we grow in victory over despair and surrender. These experiences, lived in patience, build hope. Add the Holy Spirit to this mix, and our hearts and minds grow strong in the quiet glory of living life with God, no matter what we face.

The apostle James takes this application of joyful patience a step further, adding it to not only our trials but our temptations!

My brethren, count it all joy when you fall into various

> temptations; knowing *this*, that the trying of your faith
> works patience. But let patience have her perfect work,
> that you may be perfect and entire, wanting nothing.
>   1 James 1:3-4; KJV

Amazingly, James encourages us not to despair or condemn ourselves when we are tempted by unwanted urges and thoughts we know are incompatible with God's heart and mind. Rather, he sees these temptations as our opportunities to become perfect! And the key to that victory is found in the magic created by being patient with ourselves and our weaknesses and those of others.

Let's not let our weaknesses or the cares and riches and pleasures of this life choke off our love for God's companionship in our hearts and minds, and our love and care for others. These are the values that live on forever and make our soul glad and peaceful.

8

The Fruit of Faith

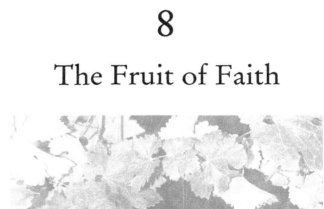

The Nature of Faith

Faith has three qualities. *One* is trust, as in "I have faith in God and His promises." Another is loyalty, as in "She is faithful to God's way." And another is belief, as in "He has faith that spiritual powers will help him."

The Unseen Powers

Edgar Cayce had much to say about these unseen powers. Here are a few of his comments.

> In giving the interpretations of these records for this entity, these are chosen with the intent as to arouse within the heart and soul of the entity those latent forces, those latent powers that may take hold upon infinity itself.

Thus may this entity become that power, that influence for the *glory* of *Truth*, for the development of self; that it may take its place, not only in the affairs and activities of a crying, weeping world, but that it may fulfil that purpose whereunto it has been called into experience and activity.

There becomes then, in the interpretation, those influences or forces as indications, or signposts, as it were, along the way. Just as the entity may look about self and find itself a part of a heterogeneous mass of humanity, with thoughts, purposes and desires for self-expression—each desiring to make itself felt and yet knowing little of why it is in that position, socially, morally, materially or politically in which it may find itself.

As it views itself into the worlds about itself, it recognizes not only that it is a part of this material manifestation of individual entities but a part of a universal consciousness of *worlds* apparently without end.

Yet it realizes there is a chord in thought, in purpose, in that intangible something that makes it aware of its desires that may not be answered by the material things; and realizing that the greater influences or forces are the unseen powers that are within the ken of its own consciousness.   EC 1776-1

Here's another:

As is conceded, even by the most pessimistic that *unseen* forces are the more powerful than those seen—or realities, as to some. The dreamer, the visionary, those who attune themselves to the infinite, the more often they receive the more infinite power, for those attunements that will bring into being those as of the realities of the *unseen* forces being as *coordinant* in their activity, as the night follows the day, the moon sheds its light from the activity of the giver of light, the sun.   EC 262-8

And another addresses the channels through which we each get wisdom and guidance.

Train, then, those activities in that direction that the spirit of truth may pervade, may direct, may be the choice of the entity in its dealings with its fellow man. For as the periods of development in the years of activity come in a material sense, greater will be the urges from the *unseen forces* in the experiences of the entity; not only in the imaginative and the impulses from the emotions, but visions and dreams will be the channels through which much may come to the entity's activities.

EC 324-5; italics mine

Notice Cayce's explanation that these unseen influences often come through imagination and impulses from emotions, visions, and dreams. These are the channels of inner guidance, inner vision. In the previous discourse (262-8), he added that these unseen influences may be gained by "those who attune themselves to the infinite." How is this done? Cayce identifies the practice of meditation, especially "deep" meditation, as well as inner listening and sensitivity to subtle feelings, even bodily reactions (that old "gut feeling" or unexplained fear or elation).

Given that Jesus taught that the kingdom of God is *within* us, then we can perceive how inner, unseen influences may be coming from a higher, more powerful place. Therefore, the unseen forces are indeed greater than the seen. Here's that teaching by Jesus:

The Kingdom of God doesn't come with observation; neither will they say, "Look, here!" or, "Look, there!" for behold, the Kingdom of God is within you.

Luke 17:20-21; WEB

Faith in the inner, unseen forces nourishes the Spirit in the womb of one's consciousness.

Faith in the Scriptures

Finding references to faith in the Scriptures is complicated by translations and interpretations of words. For example, the first possible reference to faith in the Scriptures may be found in Genesis 15:6, but each

Bible translates the Hebrew word for *faith* in various ways. Let's begin with the Bible in basic English: "And he [Abram, later Abraham] had *faith* in the Lord, and it was put to his account as righteousness." (Brackets and italics mine) The King James Version translates the word as "believed": "And he *believed* in the Lord; and he counted it to him for righteousness."

> The disciples came to Jesus privately, and said, "Why weren't we able to cast it out?"
>
> He said to them, "Because of your unbelief. For most assuredly I tell you, if you have faith as a grain of mustard seed, you will tell this mountain, 'Move from here to there,' and it will move; and nothing will be impossible for you.
>
> But this kind doesn't go out except by prayer and fasting.
>
> Matthew 17:19-21; WEB

Cayce's guidance says that this type of fasting is not abstention from food but is "Laying aside your own concept of *how* or *what* should be done at this period, and let the Spirit guide. Get the truth of fasting! (EC 295-6)

Examples of Faith

One of the most famous and disconcerting passages on faith is written in the New Testament.

> When he came into Capernaum, a centurion [a Roman soldier in charge of one hundred men] came to him, asking him, and saying, "Lord, my servant lies in the house paralyzed, grievously tormented."
>
> Jesus said to him, "I will come and heal him."
>
> The centurion answered, "Lord, I'm not worthy for you to come under my roof. Just say the word, and my servant will be healed. For I am also a man under

authority, having under myself soldiers. I tell this one, 'Go,' and he goes; and tell another, 'Come,' and he comes; and tell my servant, 'Do this,' and he does it."

When Jesus heard it, he marveled, and said to those who followed, "Most assuredly I tell you, I haven't found so great a faith, not even in Israel. I tell you that many will come from the east and the west, and will sit down with Abraham, Isaac, and Jacob in the Kingdom of Heaven, but the children of the kingdom will be thrown out into the outer darkness. There will be weeping and the gnashing of teeth."

Jesus said to the centurion, "Go your way. Let it be done for you as you have believed." His servant was healed in that hour.

Matthew 8:5-13, WEB; brackets mine

There are also many examples of Jesus attributing a healing to the faith of the one seeking healing, even to the friends of one seeking healing. Here are some of those examples.

A woman who had an issue of blood for twelve years came behind him, and touched the tassels of his garment;

for she said within herself, "If I just touch his garment, I will be made well."

But Jesus, turning around and seeing her, said, "Daughter, cheer up! Your faith has made you well." And the woman was made well from that hour.

Matthew 9:20-22; WEB

As Jesus passed by from there, two blind men followed him, calling out and saying, "Have mercy on us, son of David!"

When he had come into the house, the blind men came to him. Jesus said to them, "Do you believe that I am able to do this?"

They told him, "Yes, Lord."

Then he touched their eyes, saying, "According to your faith be it done to you."

Their eyes were opened.

Matthew 9:27-30; WEB

Behold, a Canaanite woman came out from those borders, and cried, saying, "Have mercy on me, Lord, you son of David! My daughter is severely demonized!"

But he answered her not a word. His disciples came and begged him, saying, "Send her away; for she cries after us."

But he answered, "I wasn't sent to anyone but the lost sheep of the house of Israel."

But she came and worshiped him, saying, "Lord, help me."

But he answered, "It is not appropriate to take the children's bread and throw it to the dogs."

But she said, "Yes, Lord, but even the dogs eat the crumbs which fall from their masters' table."

Then Jesus answered her, "Woman, great is your faith! Be it done to you even as you desire." And her daughter was healed from that hour.

Matthew 15:22-28; WEB

After he had sent the multitudes away, he went up into the mountain by himself to pray. When evening had come, he was there alone.

But the boat was now in the middle of the sea, distressed by the waves, for the wind was contrary.

In the fourth watch of the night, Jesus came to them, walking on the sea.

When the disciples saw him walking on the sea, they were troubled, saying, "It's a ghost!" and they cried out for fear.

But immediately Jesus spoke to them, saying "Cheer up! I AM! Don't be afraid."

Peter answered him and said, "Lord, if it is you, command me to come to you on the waters."

He said, "Come!"

Peter stepped down from the boat, and walked on the waters to come to Jesus.

But when he saw that the wind was strong, he was afraid, and beginning to sink, he cried out, saying, "Lord, save me!"

Immediately Jesus stretched out his hand, took hold of him, and said to him, "You of little faith, why did you doubt?"

Matthew 14:23-31; WEB

When he entered again into Capernaum after some days, it was heard that he was in the house.

Immediately many were gathered together, so that there was no more room, not even around the door; and he spoke the word to them.

Four people came, carrying a paralytic to him.

When they could not come near to him for the crowd, they removed the roof where he was. When they had broken it up, they let down the mat that the paralytic was lying on.

Jesus, seeing their faith, said to the paralytic, "Son, your sins are forgiven you."

But there were some of the scribes sitting there, and reasoning in their hearts,

"Why does this man speak blasphemies like that? Who can forgive sins but God alone?"

Immediately Jesus, perceiving in his spirit that they so reasoned within themselves, said to them, "Why do you reason these things in your hearts?

"Which is easier, to tell the paralytic, 'Your sins are forgiven,' or to say, 'Arise, and take up your bed, and walk?'

"But that you may know that the Son of Man has

authority on earth to forgive sins—he said to the paralytic—'I tell you, arise, take up your mat, and go to your
house.'"

He arose, and immediately took up the mat, and went
out in front of them all; so that they were all amazed, and
glorified God, saying, "We never saw anything like this!"
Mark 2:1-12; WEB

Kicking Against the Thorns

One of the greatest benefits of practicing faith is avoiding our human
tendency to kick against the thorns of life. Here are a few of Edgar
Cayce's comments on this.

Listen more often to the voice within, kick not against those
things that seem to hinder, for whom the Lord loveth He
chasteneth and purgeth every one. Be you, then, faithful in the
little things of life and He will crown your efforts with contentment, with joy, with life, with love.   EC 281-17

Kick not against the pricks that would make of life a burden in
many ways, but rather know that wholly trusting, wholly faith,
wholly understanding may come in Him.   EC 1916-5

The way of the Cross is light. Though it may have its crown of
thorns, it has also its glory that passes understanding in the finite
mind. Yet, as the infinite opens the way the thorns become less
and the way the brighter.   EC 262-37

Sing a joyful song unto your Lord and your Redeemer, who hath
strengthened you in the hours of trial, of test, of tribulation; for they
that meet their troubles, their sorrows, with *joy* in the Name of
the Lord shall not be troubled again. They that kick against the
pricks find that they but entangle their own mental minds, their
own consciousnesses in the turmoils of the flesh. You *live* in the
flesh, yet be as He–in the world yet not *of* the world; for all

> strength, all power, all glory, all joy is given unto Him—for *He* has
> overcome, and you may in Him overcome also.   262-72

An interesting aspect of Cayce's teachings on faith is that he perceived virtue as a fruit of faith. (262–18) As one lives in faith, one's heart
and mind become increasingly virtuous. He added that a virtuous heart
and mind are a fertile field for a spiritual understanding about self and
life. This understanding would naturally arise with one whose faith gives
life to virtue, which in turn gives life to a greater understanding.

9

The Fruit of Meekness

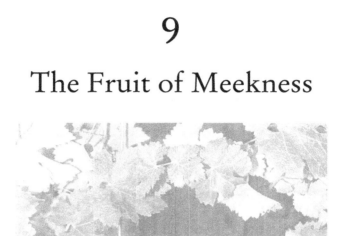

People often associate meekness with humility, submissiveness, patience, and long-suffering. And many associate it with negative qualities, such as docility, spinelessness, acquiescence, resignation, spiritlessness, and weakness. So often the world sees weakness, while the heavens see strength. In this book, meekness—as a fruit of the Spirit—is a strength rather than a weakness.

"Blessed are the meek, for they shall inherit the earth." (Matthew 5:5).

The New Testament was written in Greek, and "meek" is from the Greek word *praus*. This word does not imply weakness but "power brought under control." For example, the ancient Greeks used the word to describe a wild horse tamed to the bridle. Therefore, we may interpret Jesus' prophecy to mean that those who subdue their wills to God's will shall inherit the earth, for the earth and all that is in it belong to God.

We might also consider meekness to be a disposition that renders one approachable by all. Meekness does not exalt one's own value or position or place over another's. This would correlate meekness with respect and courteous regard for others—despite their outer circumstance or appearance. Meekness would not judge others and certainly not assume to know the worthiness of another. This meekness comes from a perception of oneness and an attitude of cooperation and consideration for all life and all of God's creation—even when free-willed beings have misused their freedom or lost their awareness of the greater truths. Meekness respects the original perfection and the ultimate potential of every being to reach its ideal destiny. Again, the meek, in this sense, believe God has a plan that ultimately leads to health, happiness, and togetherness for all.

The biblical Job expressed this meekness and faith after Satan had tested him mightily:

> Then Job arose, and rent his mantle, and shaved his head, and fell down upon the ground, and worshipped. And he said, "Naked came I out of my mother's womb, and naked shall I return. The Lord gave, and the Lord has taken away; blessed be the name of the Lord."
>
> Job 1:20-21

We find the same respect for God's way in David, who became one of the greatest biblical kings:

> Now when Saul [the acting king] came back from fighting the Philistines, news was given him that David [God's chosen king] was in the waste land of En-gedi.
>
> Then Saul took three thousand of the best men out of all Israel, and went in search of David and his men on the rocks of the mountain goats. And on the way he came to a place where sheep were kept, where there was a hollow in the rock; and Saul went in for a private purpose.
>
> Now David and his men were in the deepest part of this hollow. And David's men said to him, "Now is the time when the Lord says to you, 'I will give up your hater into your hands to do with him whatever seems good to

you.'" Then David, getting up, took the skirt of Saul's robe in his hand, cutting off the end of it without his knowledge. And later, David was full of regret for cutting off Saul's skirt. And David said to his men, "Before the Lord, never let it be said that my hand was lifted up against my lord, the man of the Lord's selection, for the Lord's holy oil has been put on him." So with these words David kept his servants back, and did not let them make an attack on Saul.

And Saul got up and went on his way. And after that David came out of the hollow rock, and crying after Saul said, "My lord the king." And when Saul gave a look back, David went down on his face and gave him honor. And David said to Saul, "Why do you give any attention to those who say that it is my desire to do you wrong? Look! You have seen today how the Lord gave you up into my hands even now in the hollow of the rocks, and some would have had me put you to death, but I had pity on you, for I said, 'Never will my hand be lifted up against my lord, who has been marked with the holy oil.' And see, my father, see the skirt of your robe in my hand, for the fact that I took off the skirt of your robe and did not put you to death is witness that I have no evil purpose, and I have done you no wrong, though you are waiting for my life to take it. May the Lord be judge between me and you, and may the Lord give me my rights against you, but my hand will never be lifted up against you. There is an old saying, 'From the evil-doer comes evil,' but my hand will never be lifted up against you."

                    1 Samuel 24:1-13; brackets mine

David bridled his will to God's and would not kill even he who sought, for no good reason, to kill David.

In another biblical scene, the meekness and bravery of one Abigail spared David from bringing a terrible reproach upon his name by killing her surly and mean husband, Nabal, even though he may have

deserved it, for, when David became king, this action would have been
brought against him.

> And when Abigail saw David, she hasted, and lighted off
> the donkey, and fell before David on her face, and bowed
> herself to the ground, and fell at his feet, and said, "Upon
> me, my lord, upon me let this iniquity [of my husband]
> fall on me, and let your handmaid, I pray you, speak in
> your audience, and hear the words of your handmaid."
>
> And David said to Abigail, "Blessed be the Lord God
> of Israel, which sent you this day to meet me. And blessed
> be your advice, and blessed be you, which have kept me
> this day from coming to shed blood, and from avenging
> myself with mine own hand."
>
> 1 Samuel 25: 23-24, 32-33; brackets mine

For a purpose higher than her own good, Abigail spared David's
reputation by approaching the future king and his four hundred armed
men. This is the meekness that ultimately inherits this world.

The evangelist Paul wisely wrote:
> I therefore, a prisoner for the Lord, beg you to lead a life
> worthy of the calling to which you have been called, with
> all lowliness and meekness, with patience, forbearing one
> another in love, eager to maintain the unity of the Spirit
> in the bond of peace. There is one body and one Spirit,
> just as you were called to the one hope that belongs to
> your call; one Lord, one faith, one baptism, one God and
> Father of us all, who is above all and through all and in all.
>
> Ephesians 4:1-3

Paul also wrote:
> Remind them to be submissive to rulers and authorities,
> to be obedient, to be ready for any honest work, to speak
> evil of no one, to avoid quarreling, to be gentle, and to
> show perfect courtesy toward all men. For we ourselves

were once foolish, disobedient, led astray, slaves to
various passions and pleasures, passing our days in malice
and envy, hated by men and hating one another; but
when the goodness and loving kindness of God our
Savior appeared, he saved us, not because of deeds done
by us in righteousness, but in virtue of his own mercy, by
the washing of regeneration and renewal in the Holy
Spirit, which he poured out upon us richly through Jesus
Christ our Savior, so that we might be justified by his
grace and become heirs in hope of eternal life.

Titus 3:1-7

True meekness will not speak evil of anyone.

The Bible reports the profound meekness of Moses: "Now the man
Moses was very meek, above all the men which were upon the face of
the earth." (Numbers 12:3) The Scriptures show us many examples of the
blessedness of the meekness of Moses. For example, Moses prayed for
Aaron and Miriam, his brother and sister, respectively, even when they
spoke against him: "And Miriam and Aaron spoke against Moses because of the Ethiopian woman whom he had married. And they said,
'Hath the Lord indeed spoken only by Moses? Hath he not spoken also
by us? And the Lord heard it.'" Sometime later, Miriam contracted lep-
rosy, and Aaron asked Moses to pray for her. Rather than condemn
them for judging him and speaking against him earlier, Moses immediately prayed that the Lord would be merciful—"And Moses cried unto
the Lord, saying, 'Heal her now, O God, I beseech you'" (Numbers 12:1-
13)—again revealing his meekness.

But, as with all of us from time to time, there came a time when Moses
withheld his normal meekness of anger and suffered a bruised ego.

Now there was no water for the congregation; and they
assembled themselves together against Moses and against
Aaron. And the people contended with Moses, and said,
"Would that we had died when our brethren died before
the Lord! Why have you brought the assembly of the
Lord into this wilderness, that we should die here, both

we and our cattle? And why have you made us come up out of Egypt, to bring us to this evil place? It is no place for grain, or figs, or vines, or pomegranates; and there is no water to drink." Then Moses and Aaron went from the presence of the assembly to the door of the tent of meeting [with the Lord], and fell on their faces. And the glory of the Lord appeared to them, and the Lord said to Moses, "Take the rod [his sacred staff], and assemble the congregation, you and Aaron your brother, and tell the rock before their eyes to yield its water; so you shall bring water out of the rock for them; so you shall give drink to the congregation and their cattle." And Moses took the rod from before the Lord, as he commanded him.

And Moses and Aaron gathered the assembly together before the rock, and he said to them, "Hear now, you rebels; shall we bring forth water for you out of this rock?" [Whoops. That was Moses' first mistake: it wasn't Moses and Aaron that were going to bring the water from the rock; it was the Lord! This reveals Moses' mistake with anger.] And Moses lifted up his hand and struck the rock with his rod twice; and water came forth abundantly, and the congregation drank, and their cattle. And the Lord said to Moses and Aaron, "Because you did not believe in me, to sanctify me in the eyes of the people of Israel, therefore you shall not bring this assembly into the land which I have given them." These are the waters of Meribah, where the people of Israel contended with the Lord, and he showed himself holy among them.

                                    Numbers 20:2-13; brackets mine

Meekness in dealing with others, even those who may not deserve it, is the way of the Lord. At Meribah, Moses' anger got the better of him, and his usual meekness was lost. It cost him the privilege of leading his people into the promised land of Canaan.

The blessedness of meekness is a special grace that is given from the Lord. We find that it ebbs and flows.

Jesus identified himself with meekness: "Take my yoke upon you, and learn of me; for I am meek and lowly in heart; and you shall find rest unto your souls." (Matthew 11:29)

Edgar Cayce addressed Moses' anger and Jesus' meekness:

> Let not yourself grow angry, with your own self or with others; but manifest meekness, humbleness—yes, meekness, not in being ashamed, no. For, lift up your eyes to Him, who is the way, and He will ever say as of old "Neither do I condemn you." For, when He forgives, it is also *forgotten.* Look to Him, for He may put into your activities that which will keep you daily in the way that speaks of beauty and charm, and all the waywardness and willfulness will be forgotten.   EC 2390-9

In an interesting twist, Edgar Cayce identified patience as "meekness in action" (EC 262–25), explaining that this enables individuals to become conscious of their souls' expansion and growth by living the spiritual life.

In another of Edgar Cayce's readings we find this question and answer:

> Q: Please explain "Happy are the poor in spirit, for they shall see God." Who are the poor in spirit?
>
> A: They that have not allowed and do not allow themselves to be directed by other influences than that of the Godly-Force itself; they that are not acquainted with the familiar spirits but with the Divine; they that are meek yet proud in their meekness and their humbleness. These are they that are poor in spirit.
>
> EC 262-111

In reading 281–10, Cayce explained meekness as putting aside one's self sufficiently to become a channel of God's light and love to others. One who is meek puts aside the comments made, the contentions, the backbiting, the spitefulness, and the love of praise in order to allow God to give life to human situations, "for he who would have life must give life to others." In meekness, God, the Life Giver, can flow through us into our lives and the lives of those around us.

10

The Fruit of Humility

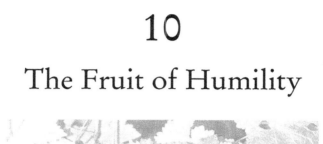

Humility is modesty, making no pretence of oneself, considering one-self not superior to others. This disposition sets us on a sound foundation, as the great Chinese philosopher Confucius wrote, "Humility is the solid foundation of all virtues."

Helen Keller, world educator on the experiences and rights of the blind, said, "I long to accomplish great and noble tasks, but it is my chief duty to accomplish humble tasks as though they were great and noble. The world is moved along, not only by the mighty shoves of its heroes, but also by the aggregate of the tiny pushes of each honest worker."

Ralph Waldo Emerson wrote: "Religion is to do right. It is to love, it is to serve, it is to think, it is to be humble."

Bruna Martinuzzi wrote: "Often, the higher people rise, the more they have accomplished, the higher the humility index. Those who achieve the most brag the least, and the more secure they are in themselves, the more humble they are. 'True merit, like a river, the deeper it is, the less noise it makes.' (Edward Frederick Halifax). We have all come across people like that and feel admiration for them."

In Psalm 25 we find: "He leads the humble in what is right, and teaches the humble his way. All the paths of the Lord are steadfast love and faithfulness, for those who keep his covenant and his testimonies."

Proverbs 11 states: "When pride comes, then comes disgrace; but with the humble is wisdom."

Among the stories of Jesus, we find this one: "At that time the disciples came to Jesus, saying, 'Who is the greatest in the kingdom of heaven?' And calling to him a child, he put him in the midst of them, and said, 'Truly, I say to you, unless you turn and become like children, you will never enter the kingdom of heaven. Whoever humbles himself like this child, he is the greatest in the kingdom of heaven.'" (Matthew 18:1–4)

Not only did Jesus teach humility, he became an example of humility in action:

> Jesus, knowing that the Father had given all things into his hands, and that he had come from God and was going to God, rose from supper, laid aside his garments, and girded himself with a towel. Then he poured water into a basin, and began to wash the disciples' feet, and to wipe them with the towel with which he was girded. He came to Simon Peter; and Peter said to him, "Lord, do you wash my feet?" Jesus answered him, "What I am doing you do not know now, but afterward you will understand." Peter said to him, "You shall never wash my feet." Jesus answered him, "If I do not wash you, you have no part in me." Simon Peter said to him, "Lord, not my feet only but also my hands and my head!" Jesus said to him, "He who has bathed does not need to wash, except for his feet, but he is clean all over; and you are clean, but not every one of you." For he knew who was to betray him; that was why he said, "You are not all clean."
>
> When he had washed their feet, and taken his gar-

> ments, and resumed his place, he said to them, "Do you
> know what I have done to you? You call me Teacher and
> Lord; and you are right, for so I am. If I then, being your
> Lord and Teacher, have washed your feet, you also ought
> to wash one another's feet. For I have given you an
> example that you also should do as I have done to you.
> Truly, truly, I say to you, a servant is not greater than his
> master; nor is he who is sent greater than he who sent him.
> If you know these things, blessed are you if you *do* them."
>
> John 13:4-17

It is one thing to know that humility is the foundation of all virtues;
it is quite another to live it in daily life among many different people
and situations. Albert Schweitzer wrote, "Example is not the main thing
in influencing others, it is the only thing."

Having spent much of my life in management, I recall a decade or so
when one of the most well-regarded business concepts was servant
leadership, a term coined by Robert K. Greenleaf in a 1970 essay. John
Bogle, the "servant leader" of Vanguard Investments, once said:

> I call servant-leadership as much as anything else, the
> golden rule. Do unto others as you would have others do
> onto you. I look at CEOs out there, probably I was this
> way a little myself, thinking they are the big cheese, they
> are what's important. But in the course of my business
> career I think arrogance took a back seat to humility. And
> my appreciation of the people that do the hard work of
> the company, those that we would call the servants
> perhaps, the people who get out of bed in the morning
> and do the world's work are the most valuable asset a
> company can have. So it's not only an idealistic strategy,
> it's a great business strategy. It really works.

Basically, servant leadership develops leaders who are humble stewards
of their organization's resources, human and financial. Jesus taught this
as well:

> You know that the rulers of the Gentiles lord it over them,
> and their high officials exercise authority over them. Let
> it not be so with you. Instead, whoever wants to become
> great among you must be your servant, and whoever
> wants to be first must be your slave—just as the Son of
> Man did not come to be served, but to serve, and to give
> his life as a ransom for many.
>
> Matthew 20:25-28; also Mark 10:42-45

Ben Franklin, a key founder of the United States, wrote: "To be humble to superiors is duty, to equals courtesy, to inferiors nobleness." True humility respects all of us, even the least among us (Luke 9:48), if not for our present condition, certainly for our potential condition, given God's power to raise his children to their full potential. The French philosopher Charles Montesquieu noted: "To become truly great, one has to stand *with* people, not above them." Edgar Cayce often quoted the old saying *There is so much good in the worst of us, and so much bad in the best of us, that it doesn't pay for any of us to think poorly of the rest of us.*

Humility is considering oneself among the congregation of God's creation—no less than anyone else, no greater. Here is where nobility blends beautifully with humility.

Here are some insights from Edgar Cayce's discourses:

> Don't think too highly of thyself. Remain humble if you would
> materially, mentally or spiritually succeed. Keep humble.
>
> EC 1962-1

> Man is in that position where he may gain the greater lesson
> from nature, and the creatures in the natural world; they each
> fulfilling their purpose, singing their song, filling the air with
> their perfume, that they too may honor and praise their Creator;
> though in their humble way in comparison to some, they each
> in their *own* humble way are fulfilling that for which they were
> called into being, reflecting—as each soul, as each man and each
> woman should do in their particular sphere—*their* concept of
> their Maker!

This is the purpose; this is the purpose the entity may find in giving its comfort, in giving the cheery word, in giving the lessons to those in all walks of life.

Fulfill your purpose in your relationship to your Maker, not to any individual, not to any group, not to any organization, not to any activity outside of self than to your Creator! EC 1391-1

Study self. Be humble, but not timid; be positive, but not in that determination of rule or ruin. But rather in that as was given—mercy, justice, patience, love, long-suffering, brotherly kindness, and forgetting those things that easily beset one in grudges or hatreds or hard feelings—but rather study others.

For your work is in directing individuals as to how things influence them in their life's work, their life's efforts, their life's hopes; and how to meet disappointments, how to meet sorrows.

For shadows and sorrows, disappointments, pass; for hope springs ever anew within the human breast. For *hope* is taking hold upon the soul that is from everlasting to everlasting!

EC 1402-1

11

The Fruit of Kindness

The only religion is kindness.   Dalai Lama

My feeling is that there is nothing in life but refraining from hurting others, and comforting those who are sad.
    Olive Schreiner, South African author and pacifist

Choose being kind over being right, and you'll be right every time.
Richard Carlson, author of *Don't Sweat the Small Stuff*

In the kindness of the activity, you show forth the love of the Father. Be not overcome of those things that would hinder, but overcome the evil with the good, and give the glory—*always*—to the Father. Keep your heart and your mind *singing* in the glory of the manifestations, of the beauty and of the glory of the Father in the earth, as you have seen manifest among men. Look not on those things that appear as stumbling blocks in the lives of others, for—as he has given of old—"I am persuaded that there is nothing in heaven nor in earth, nor in hell, that may separate man from the love of the Father and the manifestations of that love save man's own self."   EC 262-58

In the little kindnesses of the day and their cumulative effect over a lifetime, we find our better selves and our deepest happiness. Nothing manifests the Father's Spirit in the earth quite like kindness. It is warm-hearted, considerate of others, humane, and sympathetic to the many ways we get ourselves into hard and disappointing situations and conditions. A little kindness at times like these helps fellow souls to keep on keeping on.

Think of how *you* would like to be treated! Then treat the other fellow that same way! Cultivate that, and you will build a personality that may be not surpassed by any! Just meet *every*one as you would like them to meet you! In meeting a friend, a foe, an employer, a teacher, a minister, think *not* of their position but rather that *you*—as an emissary of the Lord of *Lords*—are meeting *yourself!* This is what is meant by "and your neighbor as thyself." In such a manner, in such a mien, may one build a smile that will make the whole world glad; a handshake that will make the whole world happy. These are not trite; these are *truth!* Apply them! For they are not as sayings but are practical, applicable experiences for *you*—if you will but use them!   EC 361-9

The full power of kindness is only known in doing kindness.

When you carry out acts of kindness you get a wonderful feeling inside. It is as though something inside your body responds and says, yes, this is how I ought to feel.
                                                 Harold Kushner

In the secret teachings of the Kabbalah, lovingkindness (*chesed*) is an emanation of God's being into and throughout the creation! And those who apply lovingkindness have a part of God flowing through them.

In ancient Sanskrit, the word *Mettā* means lovingkindness and is the first of the four Brahmavihāras (the Hindu virtues listed in Patanjali's *Yoga Sutras*, 1.33). Lovingkindness is also listed among the ten perfections in Buddhism. There is even a lovingkindness meditation practice designed to awaken a caring disposition for others independent of all self-interest, and it creates a warmhearted, boundless love for all life. The technique begins with lovingkindness toward oneself, then to a good friend, then to a neutral person, then to a difficult person and, finally, to the entire universe of life!

Meditating on any of the Fruits of the Spirit is an excellent way to fill one's heart, mind, and body with the vibrations and awarenesses of the Fruits, and thereby of the Spirit of God. Of course, after the meditations, one has to get up and go out and live these Fruits in daily life.

12

The Fruit of Gentleness

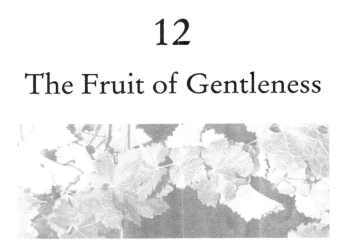

When God gave the gifts of life and free will to the newborn beings, they were free to use these gifts to express themselves with youthful, unbridled force, like bulls in the china shop of the cosmos, and many did. Jesus made this relevant comment:

> From the days of John the Baptist until now the kingdom of heaven has suffered violence, and men of violence take it by force. For all the prophets and the law prophesied until John; and if you are willing to accept it, he is Elijah who is to come.
>
> Matthew 11:12-13

Recall that Elijah was the one who found heaven and God not in the violent forces but in the "still small voice" within. (I Kings 19:12)

Gentleness is a heavenly virtue and thus not always appreciated in this world. Here power, strength, and forcefulness are often more admired than gentleness—unless, of course, you are the recipient. Everyone likes to be treated gently.

When we think of gentleness, we think of tenderness, softness, and mildness, not harshness, severity, or sternness. We do not often think of how persuasive gentleness can be or how quickly it can incline another to a favorable disposition. However, as Saint Francis de Sales once noted so rightly: "Nothing is so strong as gentleness and nothing is so gentle as real strength." And the great William Shakespeare wrote: "You gentleness shall force more than your force shall move us to gentleness." Gentleness is also among the main ingredients for healing everything from a broken heart to a broken leg.

Gentleness changes us. It causes us to touch energies and awareness that the world rarely knows:

> When you begin to touch your heart or let your heart be touched, you begin to discover that it's bottomless, that it doesn't have any resolution, that this heart is huge, vast, and limitless. You begin to discover how much warmth and gentleness is there, as well as how much space.
>
> Pema Chodron, Buddhist author and teacher

A wise Indian proverb holds that "the way to overcome the angry man is with gentleness." And that is so true.

Ralph Waldo Emerson expressed his concern that "we do not believe, or we forget, that the Holy Spirit came down, not in the shape of a vulture, but in the form of a dove." Gentleness is godly, and God chooses gentle creatures to represent his nature, such as doves and lambs. And the apostle Paul, writing to the Galatians, guided them in the ways of gentleness:

> Brethren, even if anyone is caught in any trespass, you who are spiritual, restore such a one in a spirit of gentleness.
>
> Galatians 6:1

Here are other passages:

> A gentle answer turns away wrath, but a harsh word stirs
> up anger.
>
> Proverbs 15:1

> A gentle tongue is a tree of life.
>
> Proverbs 15:4

> The author of *All I Really Need to Know I Learned in
> Kindergarten* wrote:
> All I really need to know about how to live and what
> to do and how to be I learned in kindergarten . . . Share
> everything. Play fair. Don't hit people . . . Say you're sorry
> when you hit somebody.
>
> Robert Fulghum

The gentleness lesson from kindergarten can make adult life happier.
The world is rarely gentle, but each soul that applies gentleness in daily
life offsets the world's harshness, making it a little better place to live
and learn.

Cayce's mystic insights encourage us to think, speak, and act in
gentleness:

> Your life, your heart, your body, your mind–keep them one
> with Him. Your body is the temple where you may meet the
> living God, in your trust, in your faith in Him. For He has
> promised, and His promises are sure, "As you call upon me I will
> *hear*–and will answer according to that *you* have done in your
> body towards your fellow man." If you would have friends, be
> friendly! If you would have others be kind to you, be kind to
> them! If you would know your Maker, then in gentleness of heart
> and in sureness of purpose live each day that you may look to
> Him and say, "Your will, O God, be done in me; *not* my will but
> Your will!"
>
> EC 792-1

13

The Fruit of Peace

Blessed are the peacemakers, for they shall be called the sons of God.   Matthew 5:9

Peace comes from within. Do not seek it without.
                                                    Buddha

Each one has to find his peace from within. And peace to be real must be unaffected by outside circumstances.
                                          Mahatma Gandhi

Peace is not the absence of conflict, but the ability to cope with it.   Anonymous

This is an interesting perspective on peace. It is an inner disposition that allows one to cope with outer circumstances.

Everybody today seems to be in such a terrible rush;
anxious for greater developments and greater wishes and
so on; so that children have very little time for their
parents; parents have very little time for each other; and
in the home begins the disruption of the peace of the
world.

Mother Theresa

Mother Theresa has touched on the key to peace. It begins within us,
in ourselves and in our homes. From the family home it spreads out-
ward to touch the world. Mahatma Gandhi believed that peace begins
with the children, because they are the future generation—what they
have learned when young, they will manifest when older, leading the
world.

The cynical view is that peace is that brief, glorious moment in history when everybody stands around reloading. And when we look at
the history of the world, it would seem to be so, because we rarely go
very long without a war or conflict breaking out somewhere.

Let's consider a form of peace that is rarely understood and is claimed
to be beyond understanding: "And the peace of God, which surpasses
all understanding, shall keep your hearts and minds through Christ
Jesus." (Philippians 4:7)

On June 19, 1942, in the midst of World War II, Cayce was asked to
give one of his amazing readings on the subject of world peace. His
response has as much meaning for us today as it did then. Here's that
reading:

This psychic reading given by Edgar Cayce at the office of the
Association, Arctic Crescent, Virginia Beach, Virginia, this 19th
day of June, 1942, before the Eleventh Annual Congress of the
Association, in accordance with request made by those present.

PRESENT

Edgar Cayce; Gertrude Cayce, Conductor; Gladys Davis, Steno.
Marion Wolfe, Helen Godfrey, Beverly and Riley Simmons,
Eleanor and Frances Y. Morrow, Julia Lawrence, Ruth Holland,

Ruth LeNoir, Ruth Denney, Mildred White, Evelyn Cruser, Helen Ellington, Beulah H. Emmet, Gladys Dillman, Beatrice and Richmond Seay, Sophia and Malcolm Allen, Eula Allen, Mildred Tansey, Mae Verhoeven, Evelyn R. Gimbert, Ruth Skelton, Mignon Helms, Minnie Barrett, Florence Edmonds, Lucy A. Cooney, Hannah Miller, Hugh Lynn Cayce, and others.

READING
Time of Reading 3:10 to 4:00 P. M. Eastern War Time.
GC: you will give a discourse on a spiritual and practical concept for World Peace, giving suggestions for individuals and group operations to make it effective. Then you will answer the questions that may be submitted, as I ask them:
EC: Yes, we have those interpretations that have been made by various individuals throughout time, as to what would or do constitute world peace.

In the study of the history of various groups, in their varied activities through the earth, these in the most part have sought that which would satisfy or gratify the ideas and ideals of the few—or those that were set in power from various sources, or by circumstance as had arisen in the affairs of men in varied portions of the earth.

Today we find a world at war. There is no individual but what is and will be affected by the outcome of the conflicting emotions that are prompting the activities in all the spheres of man's experience in the earth.

Then, through whom, from whence may man gather an idea, an ideal to which he—as an individual or as a group, or as a nation—may adhere with impunity; to which purpose, to which ideal, to which surety he may put his faith, his confidence?

As has been indicated, it is not in individuals or in personalities. For, these have failed—and are in the present causing those conflicts, which have set the world on fire; causing death, destruction. And fear has crept into the heart even of the elect.

Unless these days be shortened—as has been given—the very

elect may be shaken, may tremble at the destruction, the littleness to which human life is held in the ideas of groups or nations, or those purposes that have been set.

Then, there must be the looking to *Him* who has overcome the world; who hath known death, who hath known wars, who hath known trials, who hath known tribulations; who hath met man on his *own* consciousness of physical, mental and spiritual emotions; Him who hath given, "I come not to bring peace alone but a sword–to those who have forsaken the way of life"; Him– who came that man might have life more abundantly; He who, though capable of defying man, said in the hour of trial, "My hour is come–the prince of this world comes, but he hath no part in me–My peace I give unto you; not as the world knows peace, but my peace."

Then, we find, peace in the world must begin first within the heart and purpose and mind of the individual, prompted by that something which answers within–even as has been given, "My spirit bears witness with your spirit, as to whether you be the children of God or not."

As man looks upon the world today, there comes that understanding, that manner in which choice and judgments may be drawn; even as He gave to that one who had announced by the authority of the prophets, "Behold the lamb of God, that takes away the sins of the world," who comes to bring peace into the hearts of those who seek to do righteousness in the earth. And yet because he had fallen into that answering as of self to fears within, he began to doubt–as apparently no measure was being attempted, outwardly at least, to relieve him of his bonds; and he asked, "Are you He that was to come, or shall we look for another?" The Master's answer is the judgment of today, even as then. There was not the Yes or the No answer, but "Go tell John that the sick are healed, the poor have the gospel preached, the lame walk, the blind see."

Not merely the physically lame, not merely the physically blind, not merely the physically sick–but it was that which answered to the whole purpose of man's experience in the earth, which was completed in Him; that makes it possible for as many as believe to become the children of the living God.

Then, think you that you can treat your neighbor, your brother, with aught but the spirit of truth, the fruits of the spirit that He gave, and find other than that you measure out? For, with what measure you mete it is measured to you again. As you do it unto the least you do it unto your Maker.

Whose spirit, what manner of peace, then, seek you as individuals? That you may gratify the appetites of your body? That you may satisfy the lust of the eye? That you may know fame or fortune? These fade, these pass away.

Only that which enables the individual also to bear the cross, even as He, will enable that individual to know that peace which encompassed Him in such a measure that He broke the bonds of death, overcame hell and the grave, and rose in a newness of life; that you—here—and now—might know that peace in these troubled periods.

What *can* you do, then, as individuals, that this plague of war, this injustice to man be taken away—this plague of death and fear of destruction?

You may stand—even as he—between the living and the dead!

Let those that die have that purpose even as He, "It shall *not be in vain.*"

Let those that live *live* unto God; magnifying, spreading the fruits of brotherly love, kindness, patience; that this plague of war may be stayed.

You cannot pray "Peace—Peace" when there is no peace in your own heart and soul! But by knowing (for His spirit answers with your spirit) that each day, each person you meet is *glad* that you are alive! *Glad* that *you* have come in touch with them; for you have brought—and bring—hope to their lives, just in the passing!

This means, then, that you may so live the life as He emulated in the earth, that you radiate life, joy, and peace that casts out fear—by living, by being, by doing unto others, for others, that you would like others to do unto you.

O, you say, this is not new! Neither is your present distur-
bance, nor your present hope, nor *anything!* For, even as he said,
"There is nothing new under the sun." What is has been, and will
be again. Only as you *use* that birthright, that purpose, that *will*
within your own consciousness to do justice, to do right, to *love*
good, to eschew evil, may you as individuals, as a group, as a
nation, stand between the living and the dead—and *stay* the sin
that makes man make war—of any nature—against his brother.

You *are* your brother's keeper! Act that in your own heart.
Who *is* your brother? "Who is my mother? They that do the will
of the Father, the same are my mother, my sister, my brother."

If you do the things of the devil, are you not his? If you do the
things of the Lord (He is God), are you not His?

Then study to show yourself approved unto God, a workman
not ashamed, rightly dividing the words of truth, keeping *self*
unspotted from the world.

In this you may build, here a little, there a little, line upon line,
precept upon precept.

Fear and doubt cast away, trusting in the Lord. He alone can
save.

*(Q) What should be the specific form of collaboration of the members of
the Association to insure fulfillment of its purpose in the establishment
of the new World Order?*

(A) Study—each individual member—to show yourselves approved unto God. *Know,* as has so oft been indicated, oft what
may be good for one may be questionable for another. But know
that the Lord knows His own and calls them by name.

Then let each one, as a son, as a daughter of the living God,
feed His lambs, feed His sheep.

With what? The spirit of truth, the spirit of peace! *Apply* that
new commandment as He gave, "Love one another."

In all groups, all organizations, it is not what this or that name
or group may do, but as *one.* For, the Lord your God is *one!* And
the Christ, the Savior, died for all—*not* for one! No sect, no
schism, no ism, no cult. For, the first to meet the Lord in peace
was he that was also crucified. That should, in each heart, make

those who have named the Name, and who claim God as the Father, Jesus Christ as the elder brother, know that no sacrifice is too great in order that the glory, the honor of the Lord may be demonstrated, manifested among men.

What is the test? The spirit, the fruits of the spirit—that brings hope, kindness, long-suffering, patience into the experience; not merely the offering of self as one who would make of self a martyr, no. For, remember, the Lord *could*, the Lord might have kept away from the Cross. But for your sake He bore the shame, though without sin. Remember you what the thief said? "Rail not, for we but meet our own sin (or self), and He is without sin."

Then, make not of yourself a martyr, but as one that stands between the living and the dead, to glorify the Lord!

(Q) In praying, speaking, writing, members of our Association may in a small way aid in promulgating sound spiritual concepts regarding obstructions to World Peace. As some of these obstructions are mentioned, please give the basic principles upon which constructive attitudes may be based: First, Economic inequalities of nations.

(A) These are all answered in that question asked, "Art you the Christ, or must we look for another?" What was the answer? Not "Yes, I am he that you announced some three and a half years ago at Jordan," no. "Tell him the sick are healed, the blind see—" This is the answer for meeting *every* problem, every question as to the economic condition of the nations. For He gave, "Let him that hath two coats give one to another. Let him that is forced to do this or that go the whole length." These are the basic principles upon which world order, world economic, and social relations may be established, manifested among men.

For, while all have fallen short of the glory as manifested in Him, know that God—even as the Christ on the day of His crucifixion—is not a respecter of persons, nor of their employment. For, what good thing did the thief on the cross but to warn his brother thief, "We are meeting our just dues"? Recognizing his shortcomings—hoping—doing something *about* same!

Let you as individuals, as a group, and as an Association, do something *about* the problems. Not as to direct, not as to sit in high places, for no individual is in *any* place or position save by the grace of God.

Who then *can* stand before the Lord? Only those who have the pure heart, the pure purpose. To them there is peace, even in the midst of strife, even in the midst of bloodshed.

(Q) Racial hatreds?

(A) This also is answered only in that the Lord is not a respecter of persons. "He that does the will of the Father, the same is my brother, my sister, my mother." Those, to man, represent the closest relationship–blood of his own blood, materially. Then, mentally, spiritually, *do something about* those of the races that are misunderstood, or who have been neglected here or there!

(Q) Nationalism?

(A) There should be the feeling for the own self, but not unto the detriment of others. For, though He were the Son, He took upon Himself the form of man, became as naught, subject to all the trials, all the sorrows of your own self. Then, what right has any man to set state or nation above that principle of brotherly love? But always "Render unto Caesar the things that are Caesar's and unto God the things that are God's."

(Q) Religious differences?

(A) These are the swords He brought into man's material understanding. And more wars, more bloodshed has been shed over the racial and religious differences than over any other problem! These, too, must go the way of all others; and man must learn–if he will know the peace as promised by Him–that God loves those who love Him, whether they be called of this or that sect or schism or ism or cult! The Lord is *one!*

We are through for the present.   EC 3976-27

14

The Fruit of Joy

Many have had much to say about joy in the human experience. Here are a few notable comments:

> I cannot believe that the inscrutable universe turns on an axis of suffering; surely the strange beauty of the world must somewhere rest on pure joy!"
>
> Louise Bogan, American Poet Laureate

> Grief can take care of itself, but to get the full value of a joy you must have somebody to divide it with.
>
> Mark Twain

> The most profound joy has more of gravity than of gaiety in it.
>
> Michel de Montaigne, Renaissance scholar (1533-1592)

Joy is prayer—Joy is strength—Joy is love—Joy is a net of love by which you can catch souls.

> Mother Teresa

The joy of a spirit is the measure of its power.

> Ninon de Lenclos, French female philosopher and courtesan (1620-1705)

I define joy as a sustained sense of well-being and internal peace—a connection to what matters.

> Oprah Winfrey, *O Magazine*

Real joy comes not from ease or riches or from the praise of men, but from doing something worthwhile.

> Sir Wilfred Grenfell, medical missionary (1865-1940)

There is no greater joy nor greater reward than to make a fundamental difference in someone's life.

> Sister Mary Rose McGeady,
> President of Covenant House, the Manhattan-based home for runaway teens

Edgar Cayce also had much to share about this wonderful spirit of life that we call joy:

> Today, hope; today, desire. Today those things that would make you afraid are far, far away. Shadows and doubts and fears will arise in your experience, but keep before you the light of all good consciousness, of all good and perfect service to Him; and you will find that the shadows of doubt and fear will fall far behind. Let those things that cause the doubts and fears be far removed from you, through just the little kindness, the little service you may do here and there. For as you keep your mind, your body, in service that His kingdom may come in the earth, so will joy, peace, and harmony come into your experience. EC 262-121

Then do not berate self nor others for the experiences, but use them for *what they are* to bring happiness and joy into your own experience of life. And give the expressions of the experience as a portion of your contribution to the lesson in hand. For each experience is as a help, as a step to someone else. It is, if true in your spiritual life, the leaven that leavens the whole lump. It *is* as He has given, you being the channel, "Heaven and earth shall pass away but my words, my promises, my laws shall not pass away." And Happiness is as much a law as is error or goodness or day and night; for without it man is a dreary being indeed. And as has been set to song, if you will count your happiness, your blessings day by day, they are many more than that you have even any right to find fault in.   EC 262-109

Let's close with this joyful prayer:

Prayer of Joy
I dreamed that I died and I went up to heaven.
St. Peter was waiting at the top of the stairs.
He said, "You were good–

You did much that you should,
But did you enjoy the gifts God left you there?"

Did you ever find joy in the laughter of children?
Did you ever find joy in the work that you do?
Did you ever find joy in the people you cherished?
Did they ever find joy in you?

Did you ever find joy in the change of the seasons,
The touch of a lover, the smile of a friend?
Did you ever find joy where you least did expect it?
And did the joy that you feel never end?

When I awoke, I tried hard to remember
All of the words to this sweet little prayer;
something for friends when the darkness descends,
just a blessing that I'd like to share.

May you always find joy in the laughter of children.
May you always find joy in the work that you do.
May you always find joy in the people you cherished.
May they always find joy in you.

May you always find joy in the change of the seasons;
The touch of a lover, the smile of a friend
May you always find joy where you least do expect it
And may the joy that you feel never end.

And the Joy that you feel is a note in the music
Of the song that the angels sing in God's praise.
It's a song that will echo through all of creation
From the start to the end of our days.

Joe Thompson, poet and songwriter

May we all have joy in our hearts and minds as we help others find
joy in theirs.

Here are some of Edgar Cayce's visions into the power of joy in our
lives, even in the midst of difficulties and uncertainties.

> Seek the greater sustaining forces that will make for content-
> ment, peace, harmony, happiness and joy. Not in what may be
> termed the periods of turning to religious influences, but rather
> the impelling influences in self to do *something* for those that are
> aiding others to find themselves, their places, their positions in
> the scheme of things, of life, of their activities. For, as was
> experienced in that sojourn, the entity may find in the present
> that helping others to help themselves will bring joy, peace,
> happiness, contentment, and a life much worth while.
>
> EC 431-1

> Let your understanding make you strong in being more humble,
> more patient, more long-suffering with those that fear neither
> earth nor the powers in same, that regard not God nor His love
> for man's estate. In the Knowledge of Him *guide* those that are

weak, comfort those that are fearful, direct those that are doubtful. And keep your own conscience, your own mind, your own body, as one with Him. You have seen His might in the earth. You have seen the mighty fallen. You have seen the wicked arise to places of position, yet these in the Knowledge of the Father have been brought as naught or as one. For only in doing the Fruits of the Spirit may you *attain* to the use of the Knowledge and the Fruit thereof. To have love, give it; to have patience, show it; to have long-suffering, be it; to have the love of God, live close to His ways. EC 262-98

15

The Fruit of Goodness

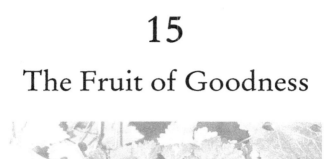

Let's give a little thought to the meaning of the word *good*. In some contexts it means positive or desirable, as in "good news." In other contexts it means beneficial, as "the sunshine was good for her." But what do we mean when we say, "She is a good person"? Does it mean that she is moral? Perhaps. Does it mean that she is righteous, that is, doing right? Perhaps. Good could mean that she is skilled, as in being a good dancer, or that she is considerate, dependable, or loyal, as in being a good friend. Her goodness could in fact be demonstrated in many ways. We could attach any one of the Fruits to her: loving, merciful, forgiving, patient, faithful, and so on.

Goodness is expressed in many ways.

Here is Edgar Cayce's discourse on the Fruit of Good and Goodness:

> Good—as virtue—must be its own reward. For, good *is*—as God

is—and *is* a law unto itself. No one may *buy* goodness. No one may sell goodness. Goodness—as godliness—is *lived*, and is first the basis of thought in an individual's inner self; and goodness does not beget self-indulgences in self in *any* direction, but is that which another—a body a soul—appreciates in whatsoever sphere of activity it may be contacted. Hence, find self in shaping self's destinies; not fates, but destinies—for 'the fates are kind' to those who love goodness for Goodness' sake, and not for payment's sake or that self may be exalted.   EC 349-13

Here are two Cayce instructions regarding good.

Keep the ways before you that are good. The Lord is your shepherd, if you will let Him guide. If you confuse yourself because of what others say, then you have not the courage of your conviction. Smile and the world will smile with you, frown and they all turn away. From where comes the smile, even though the heart be heavy? From *Good*, the *All-Good*, which is—as you know—*God!*   EC 254-9

Study to show yourself approved unto God, the God in self, the God in your own consciousness—that *is* creative in its essence; rightly divining and dividing the words of truth and light; keeping self unspotted from the world. And you become lights to those that sit in darkness, to those that wander. Though you may be reviled, revile not again. Though you may be spoken of harshly, smile—*smile!* For it is upon the river of Life that smiles are made. Not grins! No Cheshire cat activities bring other than those that are of the earth, of such natures that create in the minds and the experiences those things that become repulsive. But the smile of understanding cheers on the hearts of those who are discouraged, who are disheartened. It costs so little! It does you so much good, and lifts the burdens of so many!   EC 281-30

In the Twenty-third Psalm we find those warm words:

You prepare a table before me in the presence of my

enemies; you anoint my head with oil, my cup overflows. Surely goodness and mercy shall follow me all the days of my life; and I shall dwell in the house of the Lord forever.

Psalm 23:6-7

16

The Fruit of Temperance

Temperance is not abstinence. It is moderation and self–restraint from excessive use of any food or drink or other activity of human, sensual life. It even applies to extremes in behavior, expression, opinion, feeling, or personal conduct.

Temperance (in Greek, *sophrosyne*) is the practice of moderation. It was one of the four "cardinal" virtues held to be vital to Greek society:

1. Prudence: able to judge with regard to appropriate actions at a given time
2. Justice: proper balance between self–interest and the rights and needs of others
3. Temperance: practicing self–control, abstention, and moderation
4. Courage or Fortitude: forbearance, endurance, and ability to confront fear and uncertainty, or intimidation

These were derived initially from Plato's scheme:

> Perfect wisdom has four parts, viz., wisdom, the principle
> of doing things aright; justice, the principle of doing
> things equally in public and private; fortitude, the prin-
> ciple of not flying [from] danger, but meeting it; and
> temperance, the principle of subduing desires and living
> moderately.
>
> *Protagoras* 330b

These were then adapted by Saint Ambrose, Augustine of Hippo, and
Thomas Aquinas (*Summa Theologica* II(I).61). The cardinal (from the Latin
cardo, in the sense of a hinge) virtues are hinges upon which the gate of
moral life swings. *Cardo* also means axis, thus these virtues are the axis
around which a soul holds on to a moral life.

Not surprisingly, Temperance (XIV) is the fourteenth trump or Major
Arcana card in most traditional tarot decks.

> Temperance puts wood on the fire, meal in the barrel,
> flour in the tub, money in the purse, credit in the country,
> contentment in the house, clothes on the back, and vigor
> in the body.
>
> Benjamin Franklin

> Temperance is a tree which has for a root very little
> contentment, and for fruit, calm and peace.
>
> Buddha

> Strength and beauty are the blessings of youth; temper-
> ance, however, is the flower of old age.
>
> Democritus

Edgar Cayce and his visionary readings had much to say about the
virtue of temperance. Here are some of his key commentaries on this
fruit of the Spirit.

> [Look] not in the things of the world, either mental or material,

but rather as those *singing* of the *beauty* of the strength, of the force, of the patience, of the temperance, of the love, as makes all alive.   EC 341-36; brackets mine

From Cayce's view, temperance and the other Fruits of the Spirit transform this mundane world and life into a realm of enlightenment and soul growth, as indicated in this comment:

See how that the body, the entity the mental, the spiritual, of the entity, is given that full complete way and manner of the sustaining of the body-physical, of the mental, of the spiritual, in this mundane sphere, for first in moderation, first in temperance, first in every way and manner that *builds* to that in which the entity may gain that full knowledge, comes the truth, the way, the light, for the message will be given, and *following* in that way, the strength in the entity, in the mind, in the soul, is assured.
                                                                         EC 900-264

Cayce felt that temperance plays a major role in the spiritualization and cleansing of our bodies in order for them to be better tabernacles of God's spiritual presence with us, as in this comment:

See that peace may come *to* those who have *cleansed* their minds, their bodies, of those things that so *easily* beset, by filling same with the meditation of the heart towards *spiritual* things. Love, that begets grace. Peace, that gives understanding. Temperance that behooves the body to be crucified in those things that are *detrimental* to the understandings of the brain, and those that would succor the afflicted, those that would stand instead of those that were tempted.   EC 1742-2

When speaking of the Fruits of the Spirit, Cayce used the metaphor of a powerful seed:

Sow those same seed of constructive, creative, spiritual and mental influence that makes for the bringing of love, temper-

ance, peace, harmony, patience, brotherly love, kindness, mercy in the experiences of those who *practice* same in their lives.
                                                                    EC 1472-11

The practical application of those things, ideas, ideals that are justly called the seed of the spirit; gentleness, kindness, longsuffering, patience, brotherly love, temperance in all things.
                                                                    EC 1968-4

This seed carries the secret magic that grows a mighty tree.

The Buddha compared temperance to a tree in this famous quotation: "Temperance is a tree which has for its root contentment, and for its fruit, calm and peace."

While guiding an artist on how best to illustrate a life seal for a customer, Cayce gave these words:

In the center put (and this should roll from the right side of the drawing) the twisted cornucopia, and out of same would come rolling the seven virtues—hence seven stones, in the varied colors; from agate, the ruby, the pearl, the diamond, the amethyst, all of these colors; indicating meekness, temperance, love, faith, hope, patience, etc. upon the stones that roll from same.   EC 533-20

In attempting to help a woman who was seeking guidance on her spiritual path but was not living what she knew to do, Cayce encouraged her to get closer to those activities and energies that nourished her deeper self rather than gratify her outer self. He explained that these will go a long way toward bringing her true contentment and well-being while, at the same time, fulfilling her need for material things.

Grow in grace and in the knowledge of the truth, adding unto self those various forces of virtue, knowledge, temperance, long-suffering, patience, understanding, charity, love. All these, in their regular order. Be not unmindful that, as each is added in its own sphere and applied in self, that radiated will attract, and convince, and draw into the body that necessary to be accomplished by the body for a success. Do not look for success in dollars and cents and not in the spiritual life, for first *add* the spiritual life and *truly* all these things will be added unto you; for truly has it been said, seek the Lord while He may be found, adding unto self the various graces of the body-mind, the body-consciousness, and with these will come that success that is meted for the body. Be patient, and be long-suffering in the application—and often stand *still* and see the workings of the Lord! Do not *ever* attempt to *force* an issue! *Merit* that as would be attained by self, through meting that same element to each and every individual whom the entity may—or does—contact. Not a hard condition—not a hard element—and the body—*body*-mind—may say, "These things have I always done but they do not bring me what I desire." Take, then, an inventory of self and see if *spiritually* these have been applied in the spiritual way and manner, and *not* applied spiritual laws expecting the physical results! First obtain the spiritual response and the physical is the natural consequence of same.   EC 1982-2

Temperance in material things, both bodily and mentally, brings spiritual influences, then the material things follow in their proper order, not the other way around.

17

The Fruit of Long-Suffering

Long-suffering is enduring less than the ideal, even a disagreeable situation, while continuing to do what you feel you should do—and doing it over an extended period of time.

Long-suffering is love on trial. It enables you to forbear and forgive others (Colossians 3:13). As with the other manifestations of spiritual fruit, you can't produce it in yourself. The ability to be long-suffering comes from the Holy Spirit (Colossians 1:11) and by loving God's ways and universal laws. (Psalm 119:165) As Paul wrote in Ephesians 4:1-2, we are to live "with all lowliness and meekness, with long-suffering, for-bearing one another in love."

Peter wrote that God experiences long-suffering in patiently dealing with us and our spiritual evolution: "The Lord is not slack concerning His promise, as some men count slackness; but is long-suffering toward us, not willing that any should perish, but that all should come to re-pentance." (2 Peter 3:9)

Edgar Cayce's visions associated the energies of the heavens—the stars and planets that God put in the heavens as "signs" and are interpreted as astrological influences—with the energies of the Fruits of the Spirit. This includes the purposefulness of an incarnate life with less than ideal circumstances, even challenges. This is because the purpose is soul growth, not ideal terrestrial life and physical happiness and pleasure. When a soul faces physical challenges, whether in conditions or relationships, it gains wisdom by applying the creative thoughts and forces to resolve such problems, rather than material, earthly ones. Here's one of his readings on this matter, explaining why long–suffering is a Fruit of the Spirit.

> Venus makes for the tenderness, gentleness, the love; and yet having in same that influence in which the extremes may arise as in conjunction with the Uranian forces; so that any experience of emotional or love nature—be it material, mental or what—may be or appear to the entity as more of an experience than to many; as may the sorrow of same.
>
> Yet these are a part of the entity's experiences; so that disappointments have been as a part of the entity's experience, that have been much overcome by the application of self towards constructive or creative forces.
>
> For as is sought by this entity, and as should be the beauties of most, the application of self in a material plane is purposeful; not merely a chance but each day, each association, each activity is an opportunity for the expression of that which is the ideal of the soul.
>
> As the entity has advanced and does advance in its concept of or awareness of the creative influences within its experience, then those things that have been and are as a part of the mental self are to be met or overcome or conquered; and there is the understanding of how to use then, as it were, the tools of righteousness or of salvation in a material plane.
>
> These oft become very delicate in their nature (if words were to be used to express their influence or motivating power within the experience of an entity), yet they *are* the tools of righteousness.

> For the will is that with which each soul makes or loses the
> opportunities, which is its birthright in each experience. For He
> [God] hath not willed that any soul should perish, and it is not
> by chance that the soul is in the environ but that in the use of its
> concept of that creative force of which it is a part it is brought
> along that line, that sphere, that awareness, that consciousness
> in which it finds itself.   EC 1770-2; brackets mine

In this context, long-suffering is patient endurance for the sake of
soul growth, which is eternal, rather than temporary, material happiness, which lasts only until the body dies.

When an attitude or spirit of long-suffering is engaged—without a
"why me?" but rather with a sense of greater purpose—the circumstances
and relationship challenges of life become opportunities for developing
spiritually and mentally by applying patient, selfless long-suffering.
Also, one must not kick against the thorns of life's challenges; this only
hurts oneself. An attitude of patient endurance is the better way, with a
knowing or faith that God has a bigger plan that reaches far beyond
this one incarnation. Long-suffering is not a down-turned face, slump-
ing shoulders, and constant thoughts of how great one's burden is.
Rather, it is a cheery, ever-hopeful disposition that lives with whatever
is before it and does the best that can be done, knowing that, ultimately,
God loves us and that the Spirit is ever guiding us to true, enduring
happiness and the fullness of eternal life.

18

In the Spirit

There are two arenas in which we may transform karma to grace and apply the Fruits of the Spirit. One is the outer, daily life and interaction with others. The other is the inner world of our heart and mind and direct interaction with the presence of the Spirit. It takes practice, persistence, and patience, but if we will budget a set time and place each day, we can learn how to set aside the outer world and outer self, awaken to the inner universe and our higher self, and then make passage through dimensions of consciousness and vibrations to eventually abide in the Spirit of God.

What does the Spirit of God feel like? Like the very Fruits we have been studying and applying in our thoughts, words, and actions out here in the outer world—the Spirit of God is the spirit of love, goodness, and kindness, and so on. These are the qualities of the Spirit. In Kabbalah, these are the "emanations" of God's nearly indescribable being. By applying the Fruits and abiding in the Spirit, one comes to know

God firsthand. Meditative moments in the Spirit imbue us with the Spirit, helping our outer application, whatever the circumstances. Those moments in the Spirit are enlightening us as to the nature of God and our growing relationship with God.

Now there are two ways to experience the Spirit: One is to draw God's Spirit down to our level of consciousness; the other is to lift ourselves up to God's level. Obviously, the latter expands our consciousness and adds to our soul growth. Since a portion of our being was first made in God's image, there is a level of being within us that is a portion of God. Our little "I am" and God's great I AM meet, and the union enlivens and illuminates us. As Jesus said, "I am going to prepare a place for you, that where I am, there you may be also. And you know where I'm going and you know the way." (John 14:1-4) As Jesus taught Nicodemus, "No one ascends to heaven but he or she who first descended from it, even the son of Man who is in heaven." (John 3:13) We are not simply newly born humans trying to live our lives so that our deaths will lead us to a good afterlife. We are celestial entities that have been alive from the moment our Creator said, "Let there be Light" (Genesis 1:3); "Let us make them in our image, after our likeness" (Genesis 1:26); and "You are gods, sons and daughters of the Most High (Psalm 82:6)." We come into this incarnation with many, many karmic influences from pre-incarnation activity. We need to become aware of our life as a celestial soul, not just our life as a physical personality.

Our present reality is too terrestrial and too physical. Deep within us is a celestial soul that has existed before, exists now, and will exist after our physical death. The transition from terrestrial, self-conscious being to celestial soul and mind that is consciously one with the forces of Life and Light requires some adjustments, some breakthroughs. Meditation can help us.

A Simple but Potent Meditative Process

First, it is helpful to have some understanding of the *spiritual* anatomy of our bodies, so let's begin there.

There are seven spiritual centers in our bodies through which the life force moves along three pathways. One pathway is the central nervous system's cerebrospinal column, which follows the pathway of the spine, from the base to the center of the brain and over to the frontal lobes. The other two are in an intertwined double-helix pathway, representing the sympathetic and parasympathetic twins of our autonomic nervous system.

The seven spiritual centers have a dual nature. They are *chakras*, literally meaning "spinning wheels," of energy. They are also *padmes*, "lotuses," of illuminating "fragrance" carrying the sense of heaven. Therefore, each center may be thought of as both a physical energy wheel and a consciousness-expanding flower of illumination.

These seven spiritual centers are directly related to the seven endocrine glands within our bodies. The endocrine glands secrete hormones directly into our bloodstream, causing our bodies to change accordingly to whatever message the hormones are carrying. If we are calling on the body to raise its vibrations and reverse the flow of energy and consciousness toward the heavens and away from the earth, then the hormone message changes accordingly, helping the whole of the body achieve this goal.

Because of the transformative powers involved in meditation, there are some warnings in the Edgar Cayce readings about meditating without proper preparation and self-examination.

Warnings

> But make haste *slowly*! Prepare the body; prepare the mind, before you attempt to loosen it in such measures or manners that it may be taken hold upon by those influences that constantly seek expressions of self rather than of a living, constructive influence of a *crucified* Savior. Then, crucify desire in self; that you may be awakened to the real abilities of helpfulness that lie within your grasp. Without preparation, desires of every nature may become so accentuated as to destroy.   E.C. 2475-1

Therefore, let's examine our purposes, searching our hearts for our true passion. Do we seek cooperation and coordination with God, or are we still longing to gratify some lingering desires of our own self-interests?

The Taoist meditation teachers in the ancient texts of *The Secret of the Golden Flower* talk about the right method being like one wing of a bird, and the other wing being the right heart. The wise person must remember that the bird cannot fly with only one wing. We have to have the right method *and* the right heart. Think of the right heart as the right motivating influence.

The Ideal

The right heart concept leads us naturally to the Cayce readings' teaching that an ideal should be raised as we seek to awaken the life force. What is our ideal? To whom or what do we look for help, guidance, comfort, and healing? What standard guides us in conceiving our better selves? Who is the author of our "Book of Life"? Is it the circumstances of life? Is it our self-interests?

These are important questions from the perspective of the Cayce readings, questions that should be considered before raising the powerful life forces in this method of meditation. As the readings say, we can build a Frankenstein or a godling using basically the same meditation method. It all depends on the ideal held as the practice progresses.

> *Find* that which is to *yourself* the more certain way to your consciousness of *purifying* body and mind, before you attempt to enter into the meditation as to raise the image of that through which you are seeking to know the will or the activity of the Creative Forces; for you are *raising* in meditation actual *creation* taking place within the inner self!   EC 281-13

For those times when we find ourselves unable to "set the carnal aside" or attune to a high ideal, the readings would advise us *not* to meditate, but instead to pray. If the prayer brings about a change of heart such that the carnal forces can now be set aside, it is safe to enter into meditation. Otherwise, it is best to stay away from it. Meditation gives power to whatever is in the consciousness or desires of the person. Make sure these are pure and of the highest.

Jesus Christ

The Cayce readings present Jesus Christ as not only a high ideal but a powerful force of protection for anyone seeking to loosen the life force, to open the biospiritual seals on the spiritual centers, and enter into the presence of God. From Cayce's perspective, Jesus was a man who attuned himself to God's Spirit. Christ, according to Cayce, was not a man. Christ is the Spirit of God. Christ consciousness is the conscious awareness of God's presence with us. Cayce presents Christ as an advocate for us before the Godhead. Calling on this protection and guidance adds to our meditative process. However, the Cayce readings do not put above other religions the religion that formed around Jesus Christ. The readings are too universal for that. Seekers from any religious faith can use the power of Christ in their meditation practice and still remain loyal to their religion. Here is an example of this perspective:

> If there has been set the mark (mark meaning here the image that is raised by the individual in its imaginative and impulse force) such that it takes the form of the ideal the individual is holding as its standard to be raised to, ...then the individual (or the image) bears the mark of the Lamb, or the Christ, or the Holy One, or the Son, or any of the names we may have given to that which enables the individual to enter *through it* into the very presence of that which is the creative force from within itself; see? . . .
>
> Raising then in the inner self that image of the Christ, love of God-Consciousness, is making the body so cleansed as to be barred against all powers that would in any manner hinder.
>
> EC 218-13

Notice that "Christ" is given as equivalent to the "love of God–Consciousness." Seekers from any religion may have love of God–Consciousness. Christ in this perspective is more universal than the religion that possesses that name. Notice also that "love of God–Consciousness" cleanses us of self–interests that may hinder or harm us.

However, there is much more to this reading than ecumenism and protection. Cayce is giving us a great insight into just how a meditator may be transported from a good meditative stillness into the very presence of the Creative Force, God, with all the ramifications of such an experience. If, in our imaginative forces, we can conceive of or form the ideal (the standard) to which we seek to be raised, then we (as the Revelation states) bear the mark, or the sign, of that power (whatever name we give it) that enables us to enter through it into the very presence of God, the Creative Force, within us. Despite the power of some of the other techniques in this form of meditation, imagining the ideal is seminal to transformation. Reading 1458-1 points out our only limitation: "The entity is only limited to that it sets as its ideal." We are "gods in the making," if we can conceive of ourselves to be so, in cooperation and coordination with the Great God.

The Life Force

The life force is within the human body, the temple. Normally, it is used in ways that dissipate it, eventually leading to aging and death of the body. All of us are allowed to use our life force as we choose (at least within the parameters of our karma). Whether we dissipate it consciously or unconsciously makes no difference. When it's gone, it's gone. But it doesn't have to be this way. As the readings put it:

> . . . if there will be gained that consciousness, there need not be ever the necessity of a physical organism aging . . .
>
> Seeing this, feeling this, knowing this, you will find that not only does the body become revivified, but by the creating in every atom of its being the knowledge of the activity of this Creative Force . . . spirit, mind, body . . . are renewed.
>
> EC 1299-1

The life force—the "élan vital" of the Western world and the "kundalini" of the Eastern world—follows natural laws and can be made to flow in rejuvenative ways which enhance and extend life. This is not only possible through meditation, but it is a valuable goal to pursue. Here is one reading's statement on this:

> How is the way shown by the Master? What is the promise in Him? The last to be overcome is death. Death of what? The soul cannot die, for it is of God. The body may be revivified, rejuvenated. And it is to that end it may, the body, transcend the earth and its influence.   EC 262-85

This meditation practice works directly with the forces of life.

The most important aspect of this benefit is that it may be directed to others needing God's rejuvenating help. Through meditation, we are able to direct this life-giving energy to others.

Head and Neck Exercise

Cayce designated a specific head and neck exercise to use in preparation for meditation. It will loosen up the pathway of the life force within our bodies and get the fluids and electrical energies flowing.

To do this exercise, first tilt the head forward, chin toward the chest, three times. Feel the stretch down your back, from your upper neck all the way to your tailbone. Don't strain, but do stretch. Now, as you lift your head up so as to not to come down onto your neck bones, tilt the head backward, chin toward the ceiling, three times. Feel the stretch down the front of your body and spine. Next, tilt the head to the right shoulder, ear toward the right shoulder, three times. Feel the stretch down the left side of your body and spine. Now tilt the head to the left shoulder, ear toward the left shoulder, three times. Feel the stretch down the right side of your body and spine. Next, circle the head in a counterclockwise motion, feeling this rotation all the way down your spine; do three rotations. Finally, reverse the rotation, going clockwise, three times. Now relax and feel the whole of your spine as one vibrant system, stretched and freely flowing with healthful spinal fluid and electrochemical energy.

Prayer of Protection

Surrounding oneself with a protective prayer is fundamental to Cayce's approach to a good meditation. Upon entering meditation, he suggested, let us surround ourselves with the meaning and power of the words in our prayer. Let us then call on the higher forces to protect us from all negative influences, both internal and external (negative thoughts and emotions, etc.). Let the words of our prayer become as shields for all negative vibrations and influences. Here is a modified version of one of Cayce's prayers of protection:

> Now, as I approach the throne of power, might, grace, and mercy, I wrap about myself the protection found in the love for God-consciousness, in the thought of Christ-consciousness.

Feel the meaning and power of each word and the entire statement. *Feel* it surrounding you. *Imagine* it surrounding you. If you were completely conscious of God, nothing could move you, harm you, or distract you. Feel this. Imagine it. You may not have achieved it yet, but you can imagine what it will be like and have its power protect you. Wrap yourself up in this all–encompassing shield.

Prayer Words and the Spiritual Centers

Now let's look at the mechanics of this method. Assuming that we have crucified our selfish desires, conceived of our ideal, and drawn on the power and protection of the Christ—"love of God–Consciousness"— let's begin with prayer words for the seven chakras. These words vary with different practices, but the Cayce readings (281–29) teach that one reason the Master created the Lord's Prayer was for this purpose. As you say the prayer, feel the meaning of the italicized words as your consciousness is directed to the location of the chakra.

Our Father which art in *heaven*
(the third eye center, on our foreheads, and the pituitary gland),

Hallowed be Your *name*
(the crown chakra, on the tops of our heads, and the pineal gland);

Your kingdom come, Your *will* be done
   (the throat chakra and the thyroid gland);

On earth (torso) as it is in heaven (head).

Give us this day our daily *bread*
   (the root chakra, which is the gonads: ovaries and testes, located at the
     base of our torso)

And *forgive* us our debts
   (the solar plexus center, the adrenal glands)

As we forgive our debtors; and lead us not into *temptation*
   (the navel chakra, the cells of Leydig)

But deliver us from *evil*
   (the heart chakra, the thymus gland);

For Yours is the *kingdom*
   (the throat),

And the *power*
   (the crown of the head),

And the *glory*
   (the forehead, third eye)

For ever and ever.
Amen.

In the next reading, Cayce explained how to use this prayer:

> (Q) How should the Lord's Prayer be used in this connection?
> (A) As in feeling, as it were, the flow of the meanings of each
> portion of same throughout the body-physical. For as there is the
> response to the mental representations of all of these in the

> *mental* body, it may build into the physical body in the manner
> as He, your Lord, your Brother, so well expressed in, "I have
> bread you know not of."   EC 281-29

In one reading, Cayce gave a slightly different but interesting version
of the Lord's Prayer. I found the two phrases associated with the second
and fourth chakras to be more meaningful for me during the meditation.

> Our Father in *heaven* (forehead),
> Hallowed be your *name* (crown).
> Your kingdom come. Your *will* (throat) be done;
> As in heaven (head),
> So in earth (torso).
> Give us for tomorrow the *needs* of the body (root).
> Forget those trespasses as we *forgive* (solar plexus) those that have
>   trespassed and do trespass against us.
> Be the *guide* (navel) in the time of trouble, turmoil, and
>   temptation.
> Lead us in paths of *righteousness* (heart)
> For your *name's* (crown) sake.
> Amen.
>
>   EC 378-44; parentheses mine

To fully realize the power of this prayer, one must understand that it
is intended to call forth the highest in each chakra. Just as we felt the
words "stillness" and "God" in the earlier affirmation/mantra, so now
we must feel or imagine the change brought on by these words and
their meanings. Take your time. Consider this as part of the meditation
period.

The order of the chakra prayer is significant in that it attempts to
awaken the higher chakras before awakening the lower ones. This is the
best approach. Awakening the first chakra before the seventh and sixth
is like opening the serpent basket without the charm of the flute. The
serpent is loose to its own interests, rather than under the charm of the
higher music. Keep a higher ideal, a higher purpose, a right heart, and

your consciousness focused predominantly on the higher centers. Draw the life force upward.

Breath Power

Now once again we take hold of the breath. This time we take a stronger hold and use it in ways that arouse the life force and draw it up through the chakras of this wonderful biospiritual instrument in which we abide. Why the breath?

> *Breath* is the basis of the living organism's activity.
> . . . this opening of the centers or the raising of the life force may be brought about by certain characters of breathing; for, as indicated, the breath is power in itself; and this power may be directed . . .   EC 2475-1

Strengthening and Opening Breath

There are several breathing patterns we may use. The first is described often in the readings. To do this exercise, begin with a deep inhalation through the right nostril, filling the lungs and feeling strength! Then exhale through the mouth—this should be felt throughout the torso of the body; *strength!* After three of these, shift to inhaling through the left nostril and exhaling through the right (not through the mouth). This time, feel the opening of your centers. As you do this left-right nostril breathing, keep your focus on the third eye and crown chakra, letting the other centers open toward these two. This will not be difficult, because the sixth and seventh centers have a natural magnetism, just as the snake charmer's music.

When you have finished this breathing pattern, go through the prayer again slowly, directing your attention to each chakra as you recite the phrase and key word.

Rising and Bathing Breath

Then begin the second breathing pattern: breathe through your nostrils in a normal manner; however, with each inhalation, feel or imagine the life force being drawn up from the lower parts of the torso to the crown of the head and over into the third–eye center. Hold the breath slightly and then, as you exhale, feel or imagine the life force bathing the chakras as it descends through them to the lowest center. Pause, then inhale while again feeling or imagining the drawing upward. Repeat this cycle at a comfortable pace, using your consciousness and breath to direct the movement in synchronization with the inhalations and exhalations. As the breath and life force rise, feel or imagine how they are cleansed and purified in the higher chakras. As they descend, feel how they bathe the chakras with this purified energy. Take your time; again, consider this as part of the meditation. Do about seven cycles of inhalations and exhalations.

> These exercises [yoga breathing] are excellent . . .
>
> Thus an entity puts itself, through such an activity [yoga breathing], into association or in conjunction with all it has *ever* been or may be. For it loosens the physical consciousness to the universal consciousness . . .
>
> Thus you may constructively use that ability of spiritual attunement, which is the birthright of each soul; you may use it as a helpful influence in your experiences in the earth.
>
> EC 2475-1; brackets mine

The Rising Incantation

After doing the breathing pattern is a good time to use a rising incantation. Here is one from an ancient Egyptian mystical practice described in the readings.

Breathe in deeply; then, as you very slowly exhale, direct your consciousness to the lowest chakra and begin moving the life force upward as you chant in a drone, *ah ah ah ah ah, a a a a a, e e e e e, i i i i i, o o o o o, u u u u u, m m m m m.* Each sound is associated with a chakra. "Ah" is associated with the root chakra (Edgar Cayce reading 2072–10 states, "this is not R, but Ah"), as the *a* in *spa;* long *a* (as in *able*), with the lyden center; long *e* (as in *eve*), with the solar plexus; long *i* (as in *high*), with the heart;

o (as in *open*), with the throat; *u* (as in *true*), with the pineal; and *m* (like humming the *m* in *room*), with the third eye.

Remember that true incantation is an inner sounding that vibrates, stimulates, and lifts the life force. It is done in a droning manner, sounding a monotonous, humming tone. After vibrating the vocal cords, directing this vibration to the chakras will cause them to vibrate. Feel the chakras being tuned to the specific sound/vibration, and then carry your consciousness upward as the sound changes. Do this chanting three or more times or until you feel its effect. You may also want to finish this chanting portion of the practice with a few soundings of the great OM chant (as in *home*).

Often at this point in the meditation, the head will be drawn back, the forehead and crown may have pronounced sensations or vibrations, and the upper body and head may be gently moving back and forth or side to side or in a circular motion. These are all natural results of the practice and are identified as such in the readings. In the Revelation, St. John associates body shaking ("earthquakes") with the opening of the sixth chakra, followed by "silence in heaven" as the seventh chakra opens.

Into the Mind

Now we want to move in consciousness, so let's allow the breathing and the body to go on autopilot (the Autonomic Nervous System will watch over them).

At this point in the practice, the whole of the body, mind, and soul are aroused and alert. Now, the ideal held is the formative influence, and development proceeds according to the ideal held.

The mind has a somewhat different experience in this type of meditation than it does in the Magic Silence method. All self-initiated activity is suspended. The mind has been changing as we have raised the energies of the body. By now, it is very still yet quite alert. Stay here. Do not draw away or attempt to affect anything. Heightened expectancy and alertness are an excellent state of mind at this point. Here is where we have the greatest opportunity to receive God. Completely open your consciousness to God's. St. John says that he was "in the spirit" (the readings say this was John's way of saying that he was in meditation) and he "turned" (in consciousness) and his revelation began. St. John's word *turned* so precisely describes the cessation of all self-initiated activity. We too must reach a point in the meditation where we turn around from our constant outer-directed thought stream to become transfixed on God's consciousness, and then purely receptive.

Expansion and the Imaginative Forces

The readings say we should have a strong sense of expansion and oneness while in this state. They also recommend that we imagine expansion as we progress toward this place in the meditation. The imaginative forces should be used to help us reach higher consciousness. So, imagine expansion as you raise the life force in the early stages of the practice. According to the readings, the pineal gland's primary functioning is "the impulse or imaginative" force. It is the crown chakra that aids in the transition from heightened material consciousness to real spiritual consciousness. Use your imaginative forces to aid in this transition. Also, reading 294-141 adds, "Keep the pineal gland operating and you won't grow old; you will always be young!" Again we see the rejuvenative powers of stimulating the imagination.

The Lower and Upper Chakras

The following reading describes more of what occurs:

> The spirit and the soul is within its encasement, or its temple within the body of the individual—see? With the arousing..., it rises along that which is known as the Appian Way, or the pineal center, to the base of the brain, that it may be disseminated to those centers that give activity to the whole of the mental and physical being. It rises then to the hidden eye in the center of the brain system, or is felt in the forefront of the head, or in the place just above the real face—or bridge of nose, see?   EC 281-13

As we have seen, the soul is encased in the second chakra of the body, the lyden center. From this chakra it is drawn upward by the magnetism that results from stimulating the pineal center. It rises to the base of the brain and into the pineal center, the crown chakra.

A More Wonderful Life

The power gained from this type of meditation is not used for power but to allow more of God's influence to come into our lives and into this dimension.

We are the channels of God in this realm, if we choose to be so. We could literally transform this realm if more of us developed ourselves to be better, clearer channels of the Life Force, the Great Spirit, God. The residual effect of this is that our individual lives become more fulfilling, abundant, rejuvenated, and eternal.

Success Is in the Doing!

From the readings' perspective, "In the doing comes the understanding"—not in the talking, the reading, the believing, the knowing, or thinking . . . but in the *doing*. So come, take up your practice—not just to feel better, but that the infinite may manifest in the finite, lifting all to a more wonderful life!

At the period in the meditation in which we feel we have raised the life force and can sense God's presence with us, let us pray for and direct the energy to those who have asked for our help or who we know have need of this help or healing. Let us leave the outcome with God but do our part as channels of God's help and healing for those on our prayer list.

Why Meditate

"I just can't find time for it."
"I just don't see the value in it."
"I'm not very good at it."

Why meditate? When we feel moody, out of sorts, overworked, tired, and frustrated, why meditate? When we find ourselves whiny, angry, depressed, or weary or any of the many feelings that human life brings, why meditate? When we cannot quiet our minds because there are so many pressures, so many things that need attention, why meditate? When we are bored, why meditate? When we are sick or our loved one is sick, why meditate?

The answer to this question is both simple and complex, requiring some willpower and faith. As individuals, we have only a limited amount of energy, strength, wisdom, and power to effect change in our lives. As the Master asked, "And can any of you by worrying add a single hour to your span of life?" (Luke 12:25; RSV) In the normal, human, individual condition, the answer is, None of us. But there is another condition that we *can* get into. In the universal condition, with the spiritual influences flowing, any one of us can effect change in our lives and the lives of those around us. This is the real reason for finding time and space to meditate. By ourselves, we can do little, but as the universal forces find more presence within our minds and bodies, we become potent channels of the Life Force.

Here are a few comments about this from the Edgar Cayce readings:

> As the body-physical is purified, as the mental body is made wholly at-one with purification or purity, with the life and light within itself, healing comes, strength comes, and power comes. So may an individual effect a healing, through meditation, through attuning not just a side of the mind nor a portion of the body but the *whole*, to that at-oneness with the spiritual forces within, the gift of the life-force within *each* body.

"The gift of the life-force is within each body"—what a wonderful statement. Within each of us is a latent gift waiting to be claimed. It is claimed by purification of body, and the mind being wholly at one with purity. This correlates to the passage-in-consciousness stage in which the "earthly portions" are removed from the body and suspended above it, thereby leaving the body clear, clean, and pure so the soul can rise and the spiritual influences can penetrate the whole of our being. Then comes healing, strength, and power.

> The nearer the body of an individual draws to that attunement, or consciousness, as was in the Christ Consciousness, the nearer does the body become a channel for *life*, *living* life; to others to whom the thought is directed. Hence at such periods, these are the manifestations of the life, or the spirit, acting *through* the body.
>
> Let these remain as sacred experiences, gathering more and more of same; but remember, as such is given out, so does it come.   EC 281-24

I particularly like the explanation that many of our deep meditation experiences are the manifestations of the life or spirit acting through our bodies. After all, our bodies are atomic structures. Let's continue with the reading:

> The body-physical is an atomic structure. Each atom, each corpuscle, has within it the whole form of the universe; within its *own* structure. Each individual body must bring its own creative force in balance about each of the atomic centers in order for the resuscitating, revivifying to occur in the body. The law then is compliance with the universal spiritual influence that awakens any atomic center.   EC 281-24

It is simply a matter of natural and divine law: If we remain in the individual, human condition, then we have limited potency in dealing with life's challenges. However, if we open ourselves regularly to the "universal spiritual influence," then human conditions are tempered by these forces—forces of life and light with power to make all things new.

Meditation helps our will and choice reach accord with that of God's. Life's activities then move *with* the Divine Influence, and we can direct this helpful, healing influence to others who need it.

Time spent in the Spirit enhances our understanding, wisdom, and strength. Budgeting time for this is one of the most important activities we can do.

19

God Speaks to Us . . .

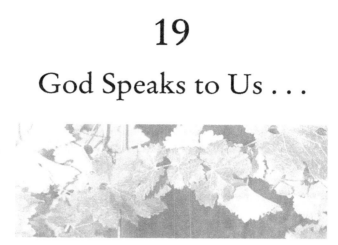

In the biblical book of Job, Job's friend Elihu states:

> God speaks once, even twice—though man regards it
> not—in a dream, in a vision of the night, when deep sleep
> falls upon man, in slumber upon the bed. Then God
> opens the ears of humans, and seals their instruction that
> He may withdraw man from his [selfish] purposes, and
> hide pride from man. He keeps back his soul from the Pit,
> and his life from perishing by the sword.
>
> Job 33:14-18; brackets mine

Sleep research centers have proven that everyone dreams, every
night! The sleep state called REM (Rapid Eye Movement) is a necessary
phase of a night's sleep and the stage in which, when awakened, par-
ticipants are inevitably found by their researchers to be dreaming. The

challenge is to bring the memory of that dream into the outer, daily consciousness.

How to Remember

Before we get into the nature of dreams, let's review some good tips for remembering them. Edgar Cayce recommends three simple things:
1. Give yourself a pre-sleep suggestion to remember your dreams.
2. Don't move your body upon waking.
3. Record the content or impressions right away.

When we are falling asleep, as we like to call it, we are actually moving from our outer conscious mind to our inner subconscious. The subconscious is always amenable to suggestion (one of the keys to hypnosis). If, as we are entering the subconscious, we are repeating a suggestion to remember our dreams, the subconscious takes that suggestion to heart. However, the body is mostly physical, and if we move it too quickly upon waking, we will jump straight out of our subconscious into our outer daily consciousness and lose the dream. Therefore, we must resist moving the body upon waking. Linger in the twilight, between the outer mind and the inner—or, as the Egyptians described it: between the land of the living and the land of the dead (sleep is the shadow of death). Here we will find our dream content and imagery.

The Importance of Dreams

Cayce realized how important it is to record our dreams and learn to comprehend and interpret them. Such an understanding can bring a much bigger vision of life to the outer person than can be gained with only outer study and application. Dreams, he said, can bring warnings and opportunities that would otherwise be lost. In fact, he said that nothing occurs in our life that is not first foreshadowed in our dreams! A journal beside the bed is his recommendation, although some of us have successfully used tape recorders (not exactly a good idea if someone sleeps beside you).

The Nature of Dreams

What are dreams? Cayce answered: "Dreams are of different natures, and have their inception from influences either in the body, in the mind, or from the realm of the soul and spirit." Therefore, one of the first steps toward interpretation of a dream is to identify the influence behind the dream: Is it the body, the mind, or the soul?

Cayce explained that the most common influence impelling dreams is "mental development." Our subconscious (mind of our soul) and our superconscious (mind of our godly self) are attempting to correlate life events and decisions with eternal, spiritual ideals and purposes. On one occasion, Cayce modified the word *correlation* to "co-relation of subconscious and superconscious forces manifesting through the developing mind of the entity." Generally, the feeling or mood that accompanies the dream reveals how our deeper soul-life feels about the outer-life events, decisions, and conditions.

Beyond the common correlating process, some dreams are about conditions in the body that need to be cared for; some deal with opportunities that need to be seized or situations that need to be avoided; others are nonphysical experiences in other dimensions of life that help us expand our consciousness. In some dreams we break the time barrier and see far into the past or into the future. The subconscious mind is like a bird high above the road we are traveling; it can see around the next bend on our path and review the distant roads we have traveled and forgotten.

Dreams are multidimensional. It is this very quality that makes them so difficult to understand. And they have a language all their own—a language of imagery, symbolism, and sometimes bizarre activity. As all who have studied their dreams can attest, dreams are often difficult to interpret and understand. Yet many humans have received life-changing insight and guidance through dreams; even major inventions have resulted from dreams. From biblical journeys with God to modern scientific breakthroughs, dreams have played a major role in the human experience.

How to Interpret Dreams

When it comes to interpretation, Cayce always said that the best interpreter of the dream is the dreamer: "You interpret dreams in yourself. Not by a dream book, not by what others say, but dreams are presented in symbols, in signs." It is important to recognize that the dreamer is our *inner* self. Therefore, the best interpreter is our inner self, so we should obtain the interpretation while still in or near the dreaming self. Trying to translate a dream later with only our outer, three-dimensional self is very difficult. It did not dream the dream. We will do much better if we keep the body and outer self still as we awaken, allowing the dream and its meaning to come from the inner self.

Here are some quick steps toward better interpretation:

1. Watch your mood upon waking. This will give you the best sense of whether the inner self is happy or unhappy about conditions.

2. Get the gist of the dream first; details second. Jesus once observed that we tend to strain for gnats while we are swallowing camels. The big picture, the overriding theme, is much more important for us to grasp than the details.

3. Understand that the subconscious may use exaggeration to get your attention. It's like the joke of how to get your mule to do something: first, you hit him as hard as you can to get his attention. In a similar manner the subconscious gets our attention: exaggerated activities and shocking imagery will do more to get our attention than sweetly whispered instructions. Therefore, don't let the dramatic exaggerations overwhelm you or cause fear. In fact, the bizarre image or activity is likely the key to interpreting the entire dream.

4. Dreams are usually symbolic. They speak in imagery that represents more than literal appearance. Like good parables or novelettes, they tell a story that has a deeper meaning than the details. Often they use figures of speech. For example, if I told you that I really put my foot in my mouth while talking with someone yesterday, you would know that I did not literally put my foot in my mouth. Dreams speak in the same manner and are best interpreted as you would figures of speech.

5. Finally, nothing will help us get better dream guidance than using dream content in our lives. Create an action plan for each dream.

Ask yourself, How can I use this dream in my life today? Even if you are not really sure of the dream's meaning, attempt to use some portion of it. In this way your inner self will be stimulated to bring more insight and guidance through the dream channel, and it will become clearer and more relevant.

Let's budget time for dream recall and interpretation, because dreams guide us to the shores of paradise. Sleep is a shadow of death and the life beyond this world. When we take dreamy sleep seriously, we learn about the heavens beyond this world and our heavenly nature beyond our physical personality.

20

Growing Together

In 1931 Edgar Cayce began to give a series of readings that outlined individual steps toward true spiritual growth. It included working together in small groups. The first group worked hand in hand with Edgar Cayce on understanding these concepts, practicing them, and writing about their experiences. They published their content in *A Search for God, Books I and II.*

Study Group #1—as they eventually called themselves—worked for years to compile twelve essays in spirituality. The first lesson was "Cooperation," and the others were assembled in sequential order before finally being published in 1942 as *A Search for God, Book I.* The group's intent was to work with the material so that it could be applied, understood, and lived in their daily lives. It was their hope that universal concepts might somehow be practically applied in such a manner as to bring a true awareness of the living Spirit into everyday life. In turn, they hoped that their relationships with those around them might somehow be positively affected through the process. The end result has been that these lessons in spirituality have been called one of the earliest and most effective tools for personal transformation introduced into the Western Hemisphere.

Although Cayce was given a Christian upbringing, his information is ecumenical. These lessons in spirituality emphasize the oneness of all life, a love and tolerance for all people, as well as a compassion and understanding for every major religion of the world. In fact, one of the most important steps to personal transformation deals with the importance of cultivating an awareness of our oneness with all other individuals. Coming to share that same understanding, Study Group #1's preface to *A Search for God, Book I* stated:

> There is nothing new here. The search for God is as old as man. This book is passed on in the hope that through it, during the trying times ahead, many may glimpse a ray of light; that in other hearts it may awaken a new hope and vision of a better world through application of His laws in daily life.

Study Group #1 was told that they could "bring light to a waiting world" and that these lessons would still be studied a hundred years into the future. Today, many decades later, this material has been studied by thousands of individuals from every walk of life and religious background, enabling them to become more aware of themselves through cooperation, personal awareness, faith, prayer and meditation, and the Fruits of the Spirit: love, kindness, understanding, forgiveness, and so on.

Study groups work with this material in small groups in individual homes all over the world. The *A Search for God* books are used as the primary text for study. Each group has it's own personality, of course, but for most groups, there are three primary focuses:

Studying and Discussing the Material. Rather than just read through the text, group members discuss their understanding of the information. Cayce insisted that everything one needs lies within self.

In this sense, each person becomes his or her own teacher and, by example, a teacher to others in the group by virtue of the results in their lives.

Selection and Practice of a Weekly Application of a Concept. Group members choose a portion of the text or an idea from the text and discussion to apply in their lives until the next meeting. Personal experiences with these efforts are then discussed at the subsequent meeting. In this way, the concepts from the readings are brought into practical application. Cayce stated that this is where the soul growth occurs, not simply by knowing, but through applying the principles in one's daily life.

Meditation and Prayer. Through group meditation, members seek greater attunement with the Universal Creative Forces. Guidelines and suggestions from the Cayce readings provide a safe framework for this activity. Prayers for others follow the meditation time. Throughout the week, personal prayer and meditation time are encouraged.

Sometimes the material studied varies, with some groups choosing to study complementary information for a time or focusing on a specific topic of interest from the Cayce readings. Regardless of the resource material or topic, the focus on higher concepts and practices for living a more soulful life, personal application in one's daily life, and meditation and prayer remain integral parts of the meeting and the weekly applications.

Most groups meet in private homes once a week, but some meet biweekly or even monthly. Meetings generally last about two hours. There is no fee for participating, although many groups collect freewill donations to help support the A.R.E. Spiritual Growth Group program, their local A.R.E. region or center activity, or local projects, such as a community food bank.

Many people who have worked with the Search for God books in a group setting have found these to be some of the benefits:

Support for personal spiritual growth
Clarification and feedback

Motivation to persevere
A safe environment in which to explore spiritual ideas

Consider becoming part of this group activity, which has served to enrich the spiritual understanding of literally thousands of people.

Finding a Group

The best way to find a group is to contact the A.R.E. Spiritual Growth Program by writing, e-mailing, or calling. See the following:

Association for Research and Enlightenment (A.R.E.)
215 67th Street
Virginia Beach VA 23451
757–428–3588
Within Canada and the U.S., 800–333–4499
are@edgarcayce.org
or studygps@edgarcayce.org
Web site: www.EdgarCayce.org

If there is no group near you, A.R.E. Study Group Services will help you get a group started if you decide to start one yourself. Here's the information on how to start a group.

Starting a Group

Sponsoring a group is an exciting opportunity. If you are new to group work, it may be helpful for you to visit a group nearby to become familiar with both the material and the group process. And, if you haven't already done so, contact your region or country representative, who can assist you in either finding a group or starting one of your own.

There are two common ways to get a group going:

1. If you and some friends are interested in starting a group, contact the A.R.E. and request the handouts that are available to assist you.

2. If you want to start a group but don't know others who might be

interested, contact the A.R.E. Study Group Department, which can assist in getting the word out to local A.R.E. members and friends in your area. You can also post notices in local newspapers and on bulletin boards of community centers, health food stores, Unity churches, and so on. Of course, using the creative power of your mind to imagine people responding to your efforts is helpful. Be positive—believe in what you are doing, and the right group of people will be drawn together.

Some Group Specifics

It is best to set a definite day, time, and location for your meetings. This allows group members to plan their schedules and to be available for this special time and work together.

Most groups meet in private homes; however, public meeting places can also be used. Many libraries, churches, and banks make rooms available without charge.

The recommended size of a study group is two to twelve people. If your initial response to a "new group" announcement is larger than anticipated, remember that initial participation in a group can be misleading. Group size fluctuates during the first several meetings until a core group emerges. If a large group of people continues to show interest, the opportunity to form a second group may present itself.

Remember that handouts are available from A.R.E. to help you navigate the group-starting process. The Study Group Department will provide these to you.

After a core group has emerged, A.R.E. requests that you complete and return a Group Affiliation form for their records. Affiliating the group allows A.R.E. to connect your group with the mainstream of all group activity and ensure that you receive mailings of regular updates and opportunities. As new seekers come to us looking for a group in your area, we can refer them to you. Now you move from a student seeking help and support to a service that helps and supports others.

I joined my first A.R.E. study group while I was attending William and Mary College in Williamsburg, Virginia. When I eventually moved to Virginia Beach, I joined another group. I spent eleven years in an A.R.E. Study Group. It laid the foundation for much of my soul search-

ing and soul growth for the rest of my life. I also spent four years in
Prayer Healing and two years in a Revelation group, studying the biblical Revelation and the Edgar Cayce readings on the Revelation. You can
get all the information on spiritual growth groups, including Search for
God Study Groups, by contacting the A.R.E. Study Group Program at
the numbers listed earlier.

21

Gifts of the Spirit

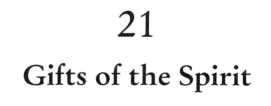

Gifts of the Spirit

Wisdom
Understanding
Counsel
Might
Knowledge
Fear of the Lord

While applying the Fruits of the Spirit, we may experience the Gifts of the Spirit, first listed in Isaiah:

> And the Spirit of the Lord shall rest upon him, the spirit of wisdom and understanding, the spirit of counsel and might, the spirit of knowledge and the fear of the Lord.
> Isaiah 11:2-3; RSV

We may view the fear of the Lord in the sense that one accepts the greater power of the forces of the Cosmos, of Nature, and God, and one's need to coordinate, cooperate, and consider these.

The Gifts of the Spirit can be thought of as powers, while the Fruits of the Spirit are considered virtues. Consider wisdom, understanding, might, and knowledge versus love, patience, kindness, and forgiveness. The Gifts are inner, personal powers. The Fruits are vibrations and dispositions that involve others; they bring us out of ourselves to interact with others (the second of the two great commandments: Love one another).

Edgar Cayce adds to our understanding of the Gifts of the Spirit in these readings for Study Group #1's course on Wisdom:

WISDOM

Cayce stated that wisdom is first an experience of each individual. It is first a choice by the individual, guided by the light of the individual's ideal, and then a matter of the will to live according to the choice made and the thoughts, words, and actions held as ideal. These become a triune experience for each soul. He goes on to give a warning: if any of the approaches to wisdom are to exalt or aggrandize self and self's own motives, then the gift is lost. Often confusion and doubt enter into the individual's heart and mind. However, if a soul pursues wisdom selflessly, seeking to exalt the source of all good and perfect gifts, then the gift of wisdom grows to a level that God's wisdom abides within the body, mind, and soul of the individual. Even the individual marvels at wisdom that comes to him or her when God's light is the guiding light, and self makes room for God.

In his course on wisdom, Cayce asked, How has He given? "You had not known sin until the Son had come and shown you the Way, the Truth." (John 15:22) Cayce continues (paraphrased):

> This is the wisdom that is shown in life, in the experience of each
> soul. It is through the variations, through those activities that
> make for thinking, analyzing, and seeking for God and God's
> wisdom that souls are brought to the closer understanding. It is
> little by little, line upon line, precept upon precept, that the

individual becomes aware of the wisdom of God. This builds, within the experience of each soul, that consciousness that in patience, in long-suffering, in brotherly love, *is wisdom!* Yet, as judged by man in the earth, these appear to be weaknesses. But the weakness of man is the wisdom of God. Just as the knowledge of God, the wisdom of God *applied* in the daily experience of individuals, becomes strength, power, beauty, love, harmony, grace, patience, and those things that—in the lives of those who are applying same—make for a life experience that is worthwhile, even in the turmoils of the earth and those activities of sin and sorrow and shame and want and degradation; as worthwhile experiences, that the glory of the Father in the Son may become known and read and seen and understood by others—that would take counsel of that you *are* in your daily activity in the earth.

The application of that which you know to do is wisdom. Making the choice, engaging your God-given gift of will and the faculties of your mind, your spirit, to direct you in your relationships is wisdom. Then, as you go about applying this, you gain wisdom—a wiser concept of your relationships with your fellow man and your relationship with your Maker. You seek, you pray, you meditate upon that God-centered ideal that guides you. For, as you meditate you feel, you see, yes, you even hear the voice, the spirit, the moving influence of God in your life. Ah, but how often when you go to apply this in your conversation with your brother, your friend, your neighbor, do you forget what manner of voice you heard, what vision you have seen, what was the higher prompting within you? For the things of the moment crowd in to such an extent that indeed we all find the spirit willing and the flesh weak.

Then wisdom is as Jesus gave during his prayerful communion with God in the garden before his arrest, "Not my will but yours, O God, be done in and through me." When this is the directing force in your thoughts, words, and actions, more and more will you experience the wisdom of the ages, the wisdom of God, the promptings of God's Spirit within you. This is wisdom.

The wisdom of the Lord your God is shown to you as exemplified and as a *pattern* for you to follow by the life of Jesus of Nazareth, Jesus the Christ. He indeed is your wisdom lived! How gave He? "If your brother strike you, turn the other cheek. If your brother seeks or takes away your coat, give him the other also. If he forces you to go one mile, go with him two." Are these but sayings? Are these but things not understood? Do you say in your heart and mind, "Yes, but He was the Son of the Father and thus had the strength that is not in me"? But you are foolish! For not only are you sons and daughters of the Father, but you have the strength in the promises of Him who is Life and Light and the Way and the Water and the Understanding! Then the practical application of the Christ-life in your daily experience is wisdom indeed.   EC 262-104

UNDERSTANDING

In Edgar Cayce's discourse on understanding, he connected virtue with understanding, saying:

... virtue and understanding deals primarily with self and self's relationship to the Creative Forces, or God, and that virtue and understanding in self is *reflected* in self, rather than a *judgment* upon another. Judge self by your understanding and your own virtue, *not* another—for these are of the spirit and must be judged by the spirit.   EC 262-19

A virtuous heart and mind is a fertile field for the growth of true understanding, understanding that comes from the Spirit of God. Cayce emphasized that understanding does not come from experience but from applying, with guidance from the Spirit, what we believe to be virtuous in our daily life. (262-18) These are his words:

measure these [daily activities and choices] by the *spiritual* aspects; *not* as man's concept from the material viewpoint, and there will come the more perfect understanding.

EC 262-19; brackets mine

As we practice the Fruits of the Spirit, we build a virtuous heart and mind and the Spirit's presence grows within us, bringing a greater understanding.

COUNSEL

Obviously, the presence of the Spirit makes for wise counsel, both within self and in interaction with others. Add to this that the Spirit of God seeks to aid all souls, not just our own—as the Spirit grows within us, it will seek to reach out to others through us, putting us in favorable position to counsel others from the gift of the Spirit within us. Whether we like it or not, seek it or not, we will find ourselves with opportunities to counsel others in their spiritual journey. When we do, it is important for us to counsel from the Spirit's perspective rather than our own, earthly perspective. This does not mean that we should no longer use common sense, no. But it does mean that we are to draw upon the wisdom gained through being in the presence of the Spirit, not by intellect or earthly wisdom, which often misleads and confuses the seeking soul. Cayce said that God will use us as counselors and advisors, but he warned us to strive to keep the Spirit of truth as the guiding influence that motivates us during these encounters. (1151-12) Cayce also taught that all souls need to find their own concept of the Creative Forces, personally coming to know the Spirit for themselves. Therefore, our gift of counsel is not for our development as authorities but as humble assistants in the awakening of the Spirit. (2132-1)

MIGHT

"Not by might nor by power, but by my Spirit, says the Lord of hosts." (Zechariah 4:6) This gift of might is that which comes from the *presence* of the Spirit and is a direct result of applying the Fruits of the Spirit in one's thinking and living. It is not the might that humankind honors and so often uses against one another. Cayce stated it this way:

> . . . not through might, not by power, not by other than the spirit of truth—which is man's own birthright, to make himself and to be one with Creative Forces or God, irrespective of those in

position or in power that feed only their own vanity or seek
gratifying of material appetites. . . .

For, the power and the might of the Spirit of truth is each
soul's, each entity's heritage—to those who put their whole trust
in Him.   EC 2556-1

Imagine the might that comes to us when the Spirit of the creator of
the entire universe is within us. There is no greater might, no more
eternal might, than God's Spirit within our heart, mind, and body.

Here is a wonderful dialogue in the Cayce readings:

Q: We are one with the flowers of the field, the waves of the sea,
the breath of the forest, with all mankind, yet different only in the
absorption or method of acquisition of the power of the whole
Spirit. We are that Spirit not yet become equal to that Spirit. The
physical is real to the senses but the physical, all of it, is but the
phenomena of the Spirit, as are we ourselves in the flesh. Then
the only real is the Spirit. To see the real we must give up the
conceived idea of life, of the conscious mind, and know ourselves as a portion of the Great Spirit, whose only happy
peaceful end is to find power, control and knowledge in this
Spirit, in God. We are God, not yet come into our heritage. Is this
all true?

A: This all true, yet the mental forces of few are able to
comprehend same in its entirety, without taking some small
portion or phase of same and running same to excess, for the
manifestations in the consciousness of the individual are the
phenomena of life. All is Life. God is God of the Living. God is
God of Force, which is of God. Now the variations as may be
seen in a physical world: We have the electronic forces in the
Universe (physical now we are speaking of), with the higher
voltage of electricity against a lower voltage, both may become
short-circuited. Now all are of a one force, one working in
opposition to another, each moving at a higher or lesser vibration (physical we are speaking of). The same applies in the
spiritual forces. All are of one, as all are in the Mind of the

Creator, all made through the Mind of the Creator, to serve in their various capacities of executing the homage, service, to the Creator. Each filling their own place. Man made to be equal to the Creator, when entering into his full heritage. Each lower kingdom made as the service for man. Man made for the service of the Creator, becoming equal to Him, or as has been presented by Liedbeter [Leadbeater, Charles Webster] in this: "Man is but a corpuscle in the Great Body of the Creator."   EC 900-89

These mind-expanding concepts hint at the potential power and might we may know when we come to the full comprehension of the One Spirit throughout all manifested life, how we may be one with that Spirit, our Creator, in whose consciousness we have our being. It is a life-giving might, not a life-taking might. It is an omnipotence that is in harmony with the whole of God's Essence, whether seen in the finite individualness or in infinite universalness.

KNOWLEDGE

Here we are speaking of the knowledge of God and God's ways, for that is the gift that comes from living with the Spirit:

The beauty of service is the understanding of the Knowledge of God. And as God is Knowledge, let that service, let that love that hath been shown you be given *in* love, in mercy, in justice, even to those that are doubters, that are fearful, that even say unkind things. For to love those only that love you, what profit hath you in the Knowledge of the law of love in the Christ? For He loved those that hated Him. He died for those that would take His life—in the earth. Then, in your Knowledge and in your love for Him, let nothing make you afraid. For the love of the Christ sustains those that put their trust in Him. And as He hath given, you shall know, you shall have Knowledge of the truth and it shall make you free indeed in Him. Then keep the faith, for Knowledge makes faith easy.   EC 262-98

Let the emptying of self make you indeed ready for the receiving
of the Knowledge of the law of the Lord. For His ways are not
past finding out to those that seek to know His face through the
Christ. Let love be without preference. Let your yeas be yea,
your nays be nay. *Know* the Lord in *all* things. For He will keep
you, if you will be guided in *every thought*, in every act, by the
Knowledge of the Lord.   EC 262-98

FEAR OF THE LORD

Thus has it oft been said, the fear of the Lord is the beginning of
wisdom.

Wisdom, then, is fear to misapply knowledge in your dealings
with thyself, your fellow man.

For as you are honest, as you are patient, as you are sincere
with yourself in your meeting with your God, your Savior, your
Christ, in your meditation, you will be in your dealings with your
fellow man.   EC 281-28

And the fear of the Lord is the beginning of the Wisdom. Not that
fear of disappointment, of contention, of strife, of fault. Consider
the thoughts of yourself even for the period you have listened
here. If you were condemned by the Christ-Consciousness,
where would your mind, your thoughts, be? For even as He
when they spat upon Him, when they condemned Him, He said
not a word; that you might know in His example, in His
experience, that you—too—would know suffering, but have a
balm in Him; you, too, would know disappointment, but have
in Him the fulfilling of all your wishes, all your desires; you, too,
would have pain, but in Him have strength and power and
might; you, too, would know suffering in body, suffering in
mind, but in Him would have strength!   EC 262-104

Cayce is wisely pointing out to us that if our very source of life condemned us for our mistakes with free will, then where would we be?
For that reason, we should emulate our Creator, our Source of Life, as
we deal with ourselves and those around us. If we do, then we become

a complement to God, a temple in which God may abide comfortably, a temple that others will find to be reflective of God and God's ways.

> . . . all this must be done in that way and manner that gives all the glory and honor of same to that Holy One, the Giver of all good and perfect gifts. Think not to bring self in that position as "I have accomplished, I will do,'" for the Spirit of Truth searches even to the joint and marrow, and the laws of the spiritual forces are even stricter than those of the secular as manifest in the physical . . .   EC 254-27

22

God: Trinity in One

If, as difficult as it may be, those of us who love God and have a personal relationship with our Creator could set those feelings aside briefly and consider God objectively, we would find that God is a fascinating concept founded upon the human belief that there is an omnipotent, omnipresent power behind all life and that it is the source of all life. Some cultures personalize this power, giving it a name, such as Zeus, or use terms that express kinship, such as Father. Others depict the power as impersonal, infinite, and unknowable, giving it no name or image. Some call it the Void, considering that there is no God-centered quality in the cosmos. In an attempt to expand humanity's understanding of God, some cultures delineate the divine power into its parts, and this is most commonly expressed as a trinity.

Let's explore the trinity concept. The first aspect of God is as the creator. This is the part that brought all things into existence. The next portion is as a helper, nourisher, and companion, one who lives near us, even among us (Emmanuel) and understands our life. And the third aspect of God's triune nature is a mystical quality that is known only through an inner, transcendental awakening and union. Perhaps the human need to express God in three forms has something to do with the three dimensions in which we have our predominate consciousness. Threes work best for us.

In Christianity, the triune aspects of God are the Father, the Son (Savior), and the Holy Spirit. Our Father created us, loves us, and seeks to have our conscious love in return. The Father sent his only Son to save us from darkness and evil by showing us the way, the truth, and the light. The Holy Spirit is our resource, bringing all things to our remembrance, referred to as the "Spirit of Truth" and the "Comforter" in the Gospel of John, chapters 14–17. It is an unseen resource that we come to know within our hearts and minds.

Although Judaism does not teach a triune God, in the Book of Formation (Sepher Yetzirah) of the Kabbalah, it is said: "God created the world through three sepharim." Genesis delineates God by three names: Elohim (chapter 1), who created light and life, and humanity in its nonphysical image; Yahweh Elohim (chapters 2–3), who created man physically, from the dust of the Earth, later separating this form into masculine and feminine, and interacted with Adam and Eve in the Garden; and then there is Yahweh (chapter 4), who interacted with Adam and Eve after the loss of the Garden. Subsequent to these names, God is called by other names, such as Adonai and Jehovah. But the first three names for God render the initial nature of God as a creator, a companion, and a resource.

In Ancient Egypt, the concept of a triune god was common. One of the most common is depicted on papyruses and wall carvings: Ra, Mut, and Amon Ra. Ra is the source of all life, and each life is a ray from this one ray. Mut is the mother and nurturer. Amon Ra is a hidden aspect of God, the unseen source of health, harmony, fertility, and the goodness of all things.

In Hinduism, we find the trinity portrayed as Brahma, Vishnu, and Shiva. Brahma is the creator; Vishnu, the preserver; and Shiva, the destroyer of ignorance and illusions. Brahma put its eternal spirit into all creation. The eternal spirit takes no form but is expressed by the life force in any form. The individual spirit of a creation is always connected to the one, omnipresent, eternal Brahma. Brahma is depicted with four heads facing in the cardinal directions, and four hands—one holding a water bottle (symbol of life), another holding prayer beads (symbol of devotion), another holding the Vedas (symbol of knowledge), and one holding a creation tool (*sruva*, a symbol of his role as creator). Vishnu, the second part of the trinity, is depicted with one head, which is surrounded by several (often seven) flared cobra heads. In his four hands are a conch shell, indicating the spread of the divine sound *OM*; a spinning disk of light, representing a chakra or spiritual center within the body and the wheel of time; a lotus, indicating enlightenment; and the mace of lordship, indicating his role. Shiva, the third portion of the triune, is most often depicted in meditation with the water of life coming out of his topknot and running upward and back to a high mountain, representing the source of original life from which we all came. A third eye, on his forehead, conveys his deeper sight. His eyes, half closed, reveal his inner attunement, and his body, covered in ashes, symbolizes life beyond death. A moon crescent is seen near his head, and the radiant sun surrounds his head like a halo, both revealing his ability to be in the source of all light (the sun) and to reflect that light when in darkness (the moon).

In Taoism—a theology of the *Way*, or *Course*—God is understood through the three pure heavens and three pure aspects of God. Yu Qing is the Jade Pure aspect of the One and is the *creator* of Heaven and Earth. In this creator aspect of God is Yuan-shi tian-zong, said to be without beginning, the most supreme of all beings, and the principle of all beingness. From him all things arose. He is eternal, limitless, and invisible. The next aspect of God is the Lord of the Way (Dao-Jun) and Supreme Master of the Way (Tian-shang dao-jun), revealing that this aspect of God is both the ruler of the way to godliness and one who has mastered the path, as well; therefore, an example for us to follow. His name is Shang Qing, indicating that he is Upper Pure, while the creator is Jade Pure (Yu Qing). He is considered to be the guardian of magical writings (Ling-bao jing). He has existed since the beginning of the world, and it is his task to calculate time, allocate it to the various epochs, and to regulate yin and yang. The third portion of the trinity is Tai Qing, the

Great Pure, and represents the immortal and divine teacher—so similar to the Christian notion of the Holy Spirit as teacher, guide, and comforter. Tai Qing will assume a great variety of forms to bring the people of the "world of dust" closer to the teachings of the Way (Tao).

The trinity is not an expression of multiple gods but an attempt to render the infinite one God in three understandable roles. These three are meant to help our three-dimensional nature better comprehend God and our relationship with God.

In Edgar Cayce's visions and discourses, the Trinity is expressed thus: "They are one; as the Father, the Son and the Holy Spirit are one." Having stated this important principle, Cayce, from his deep trance state, then separates the Trinity into three distinct parts:

> God as the Father, Creator, Maker;
> The Son as the Way, the Mind, the Activity, the Preserver;
> The Holy Spirit as the motivative force—or as the destroyer or
> the maker alive.   EC 2420-1

The first thing that strikes me after reading this is how perfectly it fits with ancient Hinduism, especially when Cayce identifies the Son with "the Preserver" and the Holy Spirit with "the destroyer." In classical Hinduism, God's three parts are these:

> Brahma, the Creator;
> Vishnu, the Preserver;
> Shiva, the Destroyer (of illusion and ignorance).

Shiva is often depicted sitting in meditation, with the water of life flowing from high on the mountaintop to a crescent moon on the crown of his head. A serpent is coiled around his neck (kundalini), a trident is in one hand (power over negative forces), and his body is covered in ashes (indicating the need to die to physical gratifications in order to awaken to spiritual resources).

In another reading, Cayce differentiates the Trinity using the microcosm of our composition: body, mind, and soul:

> Father-God is as the body, or the whole;
> Mind is as the Christ, which is the way;
> The Holy Spirit is as the soul, or—in material interpretation—
> purposes, hopes, desires.   EC 1747-5

In the macrocosm, these would likely be *Father* as the Cosmos, *Son* as the Universal Consciousness, and *Holy Spirit* as the motivative force driving the Universe.

Returning to the microcosm, Cayce tried to help us grasp the difficult concept that physical life is a shadow of spiritual life. In this next reading, he develops this idea using Genesis (Note: "These," the word beginning the first and second paragraphs, refers to the parts of the Trinity):

> These, then, in self are a shadow of the spirit of the Creative Force. Thus the Father is as the body, the mind is as the Son, and the Soul is as the Holy Spirit. For it is eternal. It has ever been and ever will be, and it is the soul made in the image of the Creator, not merely the physical or mental being but with the attributes [of the Creator]. For, as is given in the beginning: God moved and said, "Let there be light," and there was light, not the light of the sun, but rather that of which, through which, in which every soul had, has, and ever has its being. For in truth you live and love and have your being in Him.
>
> These considerations, then, each in analyzing of self, each has its part in your own physical consciousness, yes.
>   EC 5246-1; brackets mine

In another reading, Cayce approaches it this way:

> Material things are the shadows of that which is spiritual in its essence. Now you experience that H20 is water—everywhere! Then water is water, and a part of the whole, with all the essential elements that make for the ability of manifestations in bringing life, in quenching the thirst. And it becomes active thus in *whatever* sphere or phase it finds itself; whether in the frigid, as ice; in the temperate, as water; or in that phase as steam. Yet

everywhere—in *every phase*—its activities are the same!

EC 1158-12

Our physical bodies are solid matter (ice), our mental and emotional bodies are fluid (liquid), and our soul/spirit bodies are cloudlike (vapor). All three are the same—water in different forms and conditions: solid, liquid, and vapor! The Water of Life is therefore in our bodies, minds, and souls. All are here with us.

In readings 3143-1 and 5657-11, Cayce equates gaseous states with spiritual conditions and realms, noting that we came out of the gaseous condition (vapor) into matter (solid) and are now moving out of matter toward the more ethereal, vaporous, gaseous condition of spirit and soul.

How do we become more conscious of the Spirit's, the Holy Spirit's, presence within us, within our little spirits? Cayce gives us the answer, a difficult one. We may, on occasion, perceive the Spirit through our five physical senses, but the better way and therefore the one we must strive for is through "spiritual intuitive forces":

> . . . it partakes of the . . . spiritual intuitive forces as comes from close communion with the Holy Spirit, the promised Comforter, the consciousness of the Christ.   EC 262-15

The part of this reading that should catch our attention is "comes from close communion with the Holy Spirit." We need to budget time in our lives for this communion. From such communions come the all-important "spiritual intuitive forces." But this won't work if we simply attempt to *talk to* the Holy Spirit from our outer, conscious mind. We must learn to listen, I prefer *feel*, from our deep inner mind and heart the Holy Spirit's message. That is where true communion occurs.

Here it is important to understand that Cayce taught, "Christ is not a man!" "Jesus was the man," and Christ is the Spirit. (991-1) The Christ Spirit was *within* Jesus, and even Jesus credited his gifts and wisdom to this Spirit in John 14 and 15.

God's spirit with us is the *Emmanuel* (literally, "God with us") of the ancient prophecies. According to these prophecies, a *messiah* (literally, "anointed one") was to be sent from God into the Earth to awaken and bring salvation and resurrection to all souls. The disciple John begins his gospel with a poetic vision into the role and influence of this messiah. It begins, "In the beginning was the Word . . . " Actually, in the original Greek this text reads, "In the beginning was the Logos . . . " Logos means much more than the English term *word*. It means the divine, rational principle that governs and develops the universe. There is an incident in John's gospel in which Jesus actually uses two different Greek words for *word*, giving emphasis to the greater meaning behind *logos*. Jesus was in an argument with the Pharisees and scribes of the Temple and had made that famous statement, "Before Abraham was, I am." (John 8:58). Of course, he is speaking from the perspective of the Logos, through which all was made and to which Jesus is attuned. Here is his statement (John 8:43): "Why do you not understand my word [*lalian*]? It is because you cannot hear my word [*logon*, a form of *logos*]." (Brackets mine.) It is clear that Jesus is drawing a distinction between words that are in speech and the source of all expression, truth, and understanding, the Logos. Also, in the original Greek text there is no masculine pronoun in the initial sentences of the passage, therefore the text actually reads:

> In the beginning was the Logos, and the Logos was with God, and the Logos was God. This One was in the beginning with God. All things were made through this One. Without this One was not anything made that has been made. In this One was life; and the life was the light of humanity. And the light shines in the darkness; and the darkness does not apprehend it.
>
> There came a man, sent from God, whose name was John [the Baptist]. The same came as a witness, that he might bear witness to the light, that all might believe through him. He was not the light, but came that he might bear witness to the light. This was the true light, even the light that lights every person coming into the world.
>
> This One was in the world, and the world was made

through this One, and the world knew him not. This One came to his own, and they that were his own did not receive him. But as many as received him, to them gave he the right to become children of God, even to them that believe on his name: who were not born of blood, nor of the will of the flesh, nor of the will of man, but of God.

And the Logos became flesh, and dwelt among us; and we beheld its glory, glory as of the only begotten from the Father, full of grace and truth.

John 1:1-14; brackets mine

This is such an inspired opening to the most mystical of the four gospels. But another gem behind this new understanding of "the Word" is in John 8:31. Here Jesus informs us that *we* can abide in the Logos and thereby receive the truth directly and be made free: "If you abide in my Logos, then you are truly disciples of mine; and you shall know the truth, and the truth shall make you free."

According to many religions, especially ancient Hinduism, the Maker put a little of Him/Herself in each of us during the initial creation. This means that at a deep level we are gods within God, little "I ams" within the great I AM. In this way, Jesus, at a deeper level, was also the "Son of God," and we are sons and daughters of God. As Jesus stated by quoting Psalm 62, "You are gods." Like Jesus, we are both sons and daughters of "man" while, at the same time, sons and daughters of God. The human and the divine abide together in us. The great challenge is to integrate these two in the proper order.

As Cayce has said in several readings, the flow of life and wisdom begins in the *Spirit*, flows into the *Mental*, and then makes its presence visible in the *Physical*—not the other way around, as we too often believe. Let's first get in touch with the Spirit, through the Mind. Then our physical lives will change for the better, and we will be able to do more good than if we did so on our own without the Spirit.

Cayce makes this clear statement: "The Spirit is the true life." (262-29)

When we look around, we see multiplicity, diversity, and separateness. You are *there*. I am *here*. Your thoughts are *yours*; mine are *mine*. Oneness is not evident. Yet, from Edgar Cayce's trance–like connection to the Universal Consciousness, he became aware of the principle of oneness and taught oneness: "The first lesson . . . should be One—One—One—One; Oneness of God, oneness of man's relations, oneness of force, oneness of time, oneness of purpose, *oneness* in every effort—Oneness, Oneness!" From Cayce's viewpoint, one's thoughts are not one's own! In fact, he could tell exactly what someone had been thinking, because every thought leaves an impression upon the Universal Consciousness; he just happened to be one of the exceptional people who could "read" these impressions. Thoughts, to him, were indeed "things." When giving a reading for someone, he had difficulty distinguishing between thoughts and actions; for example, it was not always easy to determine whether the person he was reading for had actually done something or just thought about doing it, because one's thoughts make as strong an impression upon the Collective Consciousness as one's actions! That's a scary thought—whoops, I just made another impression upon the Collective Consciousness! It is paramount, according to Cayce, that we grasp the implications of this unavoidable oneness.

Is it possible that everyone and everything is a part of some unseen Collective, some indivisible Whole, within which all the multiplicity exists, and each affects the composition of this Collective? Cayce said, Yes: "Not only God is God," but "self is a part of that oneness." (900-181) In several readings Cayce pressed us to simply believe this, and live as if it were true! In this way we would come to know that it is indeed true.

> Let this, my children, be the lesson for you: The intent in relating to each and every individual should be to bring forth that best element in each, in *oneness* of purpose, in oneness of spirit, in oneness of mind, towards each and every one that you contact—for the individuals, in the final analysis, are one.   EC 288-19

In some manner that we don't readily perceive, all the individuals we meet and interact with each day are one—we are all one.

These are hard teachings to understand and harder to live by. We have all heard the admonition *Think before you speak*, but this level of oneness would suggest that we should *think* before we think! Does thinking negative thoughts about another person actually affect that person at some unseen level? Do these negative thoughts make a recording upon a Collective Consciousness, a recording that someone like Cayce can read? Ancient Hinduism included the concept of an *akasha*, an etheric film that records all thoughts, all words, and all actions from the first OM of Creation until the last OM of silence again. Nothing is lost. Nothing is forgotten. Nothing is unknowable. Watching Cayce give readings on the activities of celestial godlings that lived before the Earth even existed certainly suggests that nothing is forgotten or lost or unknowable. While his body was on the couch to give readings and his conscious mind was, for all intents and purposes, asleep, Cayce's deeper mind engaged. He could then tell us about long forgotten events in people's early childhoods or ancient past lives of their souls that still affected them in the present. In some cases, as an individual's reading was about to begin, he would describe seeing the person's surroundings and what the individual was doing.

In the 1960s and '70s, when meditation was taking hold in this country, meditators began to speak of experiencing a sense of oneness with all of life when they reached deeper levels of meditation. When questioned about this, all they could say was that, at some moment in their meditation, all life seemed connected. But the gap between this inner, meditative feeling and the outer sensory perception is a chasm. There is simply no outer sensory corroboration for such a position. Oneness is an inner perception. Apparently, oneness has to be experienced firsthand in order to overcome all the outer contradictions to its existence. And short of rare, miraculous epiphanies, meditation appears to be the best way to perceive the unseen oneness. Even Jesus had trouble making the oneness argument with his disciple Philip at the Last Supper, finally conceding that if he could not believe Jesus' oneness with the Father and that Philip had therefore known the Father by knowing Jesus, then let the outer miracles act as evidence of this oneness with God.

But let's press this oneness idea a little further. How can selfish or evil people still be in oneness with the Collective? And if they are, simply because there is no way to be outside of the Whole, then why are they allowed to do so much harm to others in the Collective? In a very complex discussion between one of the greatest questioners of Edgar Cayce, Morton Blumenthal, #900, and the "sleeping" Edgar Cayce, attuned to the Collective, we can find some insights into these hard questions. Since the discussion is so complex, I have paraphrased here:

Morton: On Oct. 15, Thursday, at home I had this dream: It seemed my mother and I were in a hotel where many people were passing by. Then there was a typewriter with a sheet of blank paper in it, waiting to be used by one of the many applicants for the position of stenographer. The typewriter also seemed to be waiting for my more perfect understanding of something else–some final thing–the first 3 principles of which I had two. In the midst of all of this, a voice said: "All of these are God!"

Cayce: This dream is presenting to the entity the oneness of purpose, of intent, of the whole being as one. For all is of God, see? And as the entity gains knowledge from living the various phases of oneness, he gains that first principle of which the other two he already has. That first principle is this: God is in you manifesting to other individuals through every phenomenized situation that is presented in a physical world. For, every force which may not be separated or produced by man is of God and of the Universal Forces. These are the three forces in man: (1) Spiritual–of God; (2) Cosmic–the forces made by man; and (3) Subconscious–the force that bridges the Spiritual and the Cosmic, connecting the spiritual with the cosmic.

Morton: It seems to me that this dream imagery tries again and again to drive home to my dense physical mind that God is One . . .

Cayce: (Interrupting) Correct.

Morton: God is all of these people passing in the hotel and all of the applicants for the stenographer job . . .

Cayce: (Interrupting) Correct.

Morton: All these people are phenomenized forms of God. Also God is all of these consciousnesses . . .

Cayce: (Interrupting) Except that God is not the cosmic forces made by free-will man. These are not related to spiritual forces. These are earth made.   EC 900-147

In many of his readings Cayce explained that evil is man's misuse of the gift of free will. The Creator allows this because free will is the only way for any soul to reach its original purpose for existence: To know itself to be itself yet *choose* to be one with the Whole, with the Creator and the creation. If free will is taken away, then the soul no longer has the potential to become an eternal companion with its creator. As the theological concept goes, man was made a little less than the angels but with the potential to judge even the angels. This is why souls misusing free will are allowed more time to discover their true purpose, even if they do much harm along the way. Eventually, as recorded in the Revelation, God will stop time and separate misusers from those who have tried to fulfill their purpose. For the companionable souls, He/She will then "wipe away every tear from their eyes" and set up "a new heaven and a new earth" to enjoy with God.

According to Cayce's readings and many other classic sources, before anything was created, there existed something that caused the Creation to begin. The potential for the Creation was latent in pre-Creation emptiness. Cayce often referred to this as "the first impulse, the first cause." A good way for us to grasp how there could be anything *before* the Creation is to think of the infinite emptiness as a consciousness, much like our own, except that this consciousness was infinite and perfectly still—no thoughts—quiet. Imagining this with our own minds is one of the states of meditation: a clear, quiet mind—hard to do for even a few minutes. At some moment this infinite mind began to move, to conceive, and the Creation began. Imagine how the idea of light awoke, and playing with this idea, the infinite mind conceived of stars and galaxies of all shapes, sizes, and colors. At some point in this conception process, the readings say, the Universal Consciousness conceived of companions to itself, companions made in its own image—minds—with life, creativity, and free will. Countless little minds were conceived in the one, infinite mind. At first, we (the little minds) remained consciously connected to the One Mind. But as we began to use our free wills to experience individual consciousness, we focused more on our own consciousness and gradually lost our connection with the Infinite Mind. We did not go anywhere. There was nowhere to go beyond the Whole. We simply lost consistent consciousness of our oneness with the Infinite Consciousness. Today, billions of years after it all began, we struggle to regain and retain conscious awareness of the One Mind, within which we all exist and with which we are all destined to consciously companion forever—if we choose to.

Just as this is all getting clearer, Cayce tosses a brick into our thinking when he says such mind-boggling things as "there is no time, no space." He explains that, at a deep level, there actually is no beginning, no end—all time is one—there actually is no *here* and no *there*. As demonstrated by his own readings, he could tell us what we (our deeper selves) thought eons ago as if it were yesterday, and could physically be in Virginia Beach while viewing a person in San Diego! During his readings, there was indeed no time, no space. All was one.

Cayce said it this way:

> Learn these lessons well: First, the continuity of life. There is no time; it is one time. There is no space; it is one space. There is no force, other than all force in its various phases and applications. The individual is such a part of God that one's thoughts may become crimes or miracles, for thoughts are deeds. That that one metes must be met again. That one applies will be applied again and again until that oneness of time, space, force are learned and the individual is one with the whole.
>
> EC 4341-1

Fortunately for our three-dimensional selves, he did instruct that time and space were helpful tools for developing souls to use in the day-to-day, step-by-step process of application and enlightenment. But his deeper mind cautioned against getting lost in the limitations of time and space, encouraging us to budget some time and space for experiencing the timelessness and spacelessness; in other words, the oneness.

He also instructed seekers to watch themselves go by; that is, watch themselves interact with others, watch their minds thinking about situations and people, and see if their words, actions, and thoughts reflected the truth of the oneness or the illusion of separateness, multiplicity, and diversity.

From Cayce's trance perspective, the greatest evil in the earth and in the hearts and minds of individuals is contention, faultfinding, loving of self, and loving of praise, because these forces separate. The greatest good in the world is love, patience, kindness, forgiveness, and understanding, because these forces unite.

"These are times when every effort should be made to preserve the universality of love . . . " (877-29) He instructed one person to "study the truths about oneness, whether Jewish, Gentile, Greek, or heathen!" (136-12) Among religions, Cayce said that wherever the principle of one God and one people is taught, there is truth. Further, in many of the world's great religions, the principle of oneness is there, but men have

> . . . turned this aside to meet their *own* immediate needs, . . . as a moralist or the head of any independent . . . power . . . , for "Know the Lord your God is One!" whether this is directing one of the Confucius thought, Brahman thought, Buddha thought, Mohammedan thought . . . there *is only* one. In this is built the whole law and gospel of every age that has said, "There is *one* God!"   EC 364-9

As with all these concepts, they begin within our individual minds and hearts, and since there is oneness, the more individuals believe in the oneness and live it in their lives, the more it makes an impression upon the Collective Consciousness and finds its way into other individual minds and hearts. We are the leaven that can leaven the whole loaf of humanity. Let's budget time to experience the oneness in meditation. Let's practice oneness in our thoughts about others and interactions with others. Ultimately, despite all the present indications to the contrary, humanity will come to know its oneness with one another and with the Creative Forces, Creator of all, God.

A.R.E. PRESS

Edgar Cayce (1877–1945) founded the non-profit Association for Research and Enlightenment (A.R.E.) in 1931, to explore spirituality, holistic health, intuition, dream interpretation, psychic development, reincarnation, and ancient mysteries—all subjects that frequently came up in the more than 14,000 documented psychic readings given by Cayce.

Edgar Cayce's A.R.E. provides individuals from all walks of life and a variety of religious backgrounds with tools for personal transformation and healing at all levels—body, mind, and spirit.

A.R.E. Press has been publishing since 1931 as well, with the mission of furthering the work of A.R.E. by publishing books, DVDs, and CDs to support the organization's goal of helping people to change their lives for the better physically, mentally, and spiritually.

In 2009, A.R.E. Press launched its second imprint, 4th Dimension Press. While A.R.E. Press features topics directly related to the work of Edgar Cayce and often includes excerpts from the Cayce readings, 4th Dimension Press allows us to take our publishing efforts further with like-minded and expansive explorations into the mysteries and spirituality of our existence without direct reference to Cayce specific content.

**A.R.E. Press/4th Dimension Press
215 67th Street
Virginia Beach, VA 23451**

Learn more at EdgarCayce.org. Visit ARECatalog.com to browse and purchase additional titles.

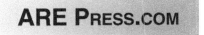

Who Was Edgar Cayce?
Twentieth Century Psychic and Medical Clairvoyant

Edgar Cayce (pronounced Kay-Cee, 1877-1945) has been called the "sleeping prophet," the "father of holistic medicine," and the most-documented psychic of the 20th century. For more than 40 years of his adult life, Cayce gave psychic "readings" to thousands of seekers while in an unconscious state, diagnosing illnesses and revealing lives lived in the past and prophecies yet to come. But who, exactly, was Edgar Cayce?

Cayce was born on a farm in Hopkinsville, Kentucky, in 1877, and his psychic abilities began to appear as early as his childhood. He was able to see and talk to his late grandfather's spirit, and often played with "imaginary friends" whom he said were spirits on the other side. He also displayed an uncanny ability to memorize the pages of a book simply by sleeping on it. These gifts labeled the young Cayce as strange, but all Cayce really wanted was to help others, especially children.

Later in life, Cayce would find that he had the ability to put himself into a sleep-like state by lying down on a couch, closing his eyes, and folding his hands over his stomach. In this state of relaxation and meditation, he was able to place his mind in contact with all time and space—the universal consciousness, also known as the super-conscious mind. From there, he could respond to questions as broad as, "What are the secrets of the universe?" and "What is my purpose in life?" to as specific as, "What can I do to help my arthritis?" and "How were the pyramids of Egypt built?" His responses to these questions came to be called "readings," and their insights offer practical help and advice to individuals even today.

The majority of Edgar Cayce's readings deal with holistic health and the treatment of illness. Yet, although best known for this material, the sleeping Cayce did not seem to be limited to concerns about the physical body. In fact, in their entirety, the readings discuss an astonishing 10,000 different topics. This vast array of subject matter can be narrowed down into a smaller group of topics that, when compiled together, deal with the following five categories: (1) Health-Related Information; (2) Philosophy and Reincarnation; (3) Dreams and Dream Interpretation; (4) ESP and Psychic Phenomena; and (5) Spiritual Growth, Meditation, and Prayer.

Learn more at EdgarCayce.org.

What Is A.R.E.?

Edgar Cayce founded the non-profit Association for Research and Enlightenment (A.R.E.) in 1931, to explore spirituality, holistic health, intuition, dream interpretation, psychic development, reincarnation, and ancient mysteries—all subjects that frequently came up in the more than 14,000 documented psychic readings given by Cayce.

The Mission of the A.R.E. is to help people transform their lives for the better, through research, education, and application of core concepts found in the Edgar Cayce readings and kindred materials that seek to manifest the love of God and all people and promote the purposefulness of life, the oneness of God, the spiritual nature of humankind, and the connection of body, mind, and spirit.

With an international headquarters in Virginia Beach, Va., a regional headquarters in Houston, regional representatives throughout the U.S., Edgar Cayce Centers in more than thirty countries, and individual members in more than seventy countries, the A.R.E. community is a global network of individuals.

A.R.E. conferences, international tours, camps for children and adults, regional activities, and study groups allow like-minded people to gather for educational and fellowship opportunities worldwide.

A.R.E. offers membership benefits and services that include a quarterly body-mind-spirit member magazine, *Venture Inward*, a member newsletter covering the major topics of the readings, and access to the entire set of readings in an exclusive online database.

Learn more at EdgarCayce.org.

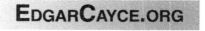